Get Out of Your Own Way

Break Free from Self-Sabotage, Silence the Inner Critic, Build Unshakable Confidence and Reclaim Your Life

Brian Chase

Contents

Introduction   1

1. The Surprising Truth About Your Inner Saboteur   4

2. Turning Your Inner Critic into Your Biggest Fan   19

3. The Procrastination Paradox: Why Delay Can Be Your Secret Weapon   35

4. Failure as Your North Star: Navigating Towards Success   51

5. The Gratitude Revolution: From Scarcity to Abundance Mindset   66

6. Mindfulness for the Skeptic: Practical Applications in a Busy World   81

7. The Nutrition-Confidence Connection You Never Knew Existed   99

8. Boundary Alchemy: Turning No into Your Greatest Yes   113

9. Your Personal Board of Directors: Curating Your Inner Circle   128

10. The 'What If' Game: Harnessing Your Imagination for Good   144

11. Action Alchemy: Turning Small Steps into Quantum Leaps   161

12. The Identity Shift: Becoming the Person You Want to Be   176

Conclusion   193

Introduction

Welcome, brave reader. You've just taken the first step on an incredible journey.

Picture this: You're standing at the edge of a vast, unexplored wilderness. The path ahead is unclear, shrouded in mist. Your heart races with a mix of excitement and fear. You know that beyond those trees lies the life you've always dreamed of - a life of confidence, purpose, and fulfillment. But something's holding you back. A little voice whispers, "You can't do this. You're not ready. You'll fail."

Sound familiar?

We've all been there. That voice? It's your inner saboteur. And it's been calling the shots for far too long.

But here's the thing: You picked up this book. That means you're ready for change. You're ready to silence that voice and step into your power. And I'm here to guide you every step of the way.

This book isn't just another self-help manual gathering dust on your shelf. It's a practical, actionable roadmap to transform your life from the inside out. Whether you're a student drowning in assignments, a professional stuck in a soul-sucking job, or an entrepreneur paralyzed by fear of failure, the tools and strategies in these pages will help you break free from self-imposed limitations and create the life you've always wanted.

So, what makes this book different?

We're going to flip the script on everything you thought you knew about self-improvement. We'll explore how your inner critic can become your biggest cheerleader, how procrastination can be a secret weapon, and why failure might just be your best guide to success.

This isn't about positive thinking or empty affirmations. We're diving deep into the latest psychological research, neuroscience, and even nutrition to uncover the hidden connections between your mindset and your actions. You'll discover how small shifts in your daily habits can lead to massive changes in your life.

But here's the real game-changer: This book is a workshop, not a lecture. You won't just read about overcoming self-doubt; you'll actively engage in exercises and strategies designed to rewire your brain for success. Each chapter builds on the last, guiding you step-by-step from self-doubt to self-assurance.

Here's a sneak peek at what you'll learn:

- How to turn your inner critic into your biggest fan (Chapter 2)

- The surprising power of strategic procrastination (Chapter 3)

- Why failure might be your best guide to success (Chapter 4)

- The unexpected link between what you eat and how confident you feel (Chapter 7)

- How to build your personal "board of directors" for unstoppable support (Chapter 9)

And that's just the tip of the iceberg.

Now, I'll be honest with you. This journey won't always be easy. We'll be challenging deep-rooted beliefs and pushing you out of your comfort zone. There will be moments when that old voice of doubt creeps back in. But I promise you this: if you commit to the process, if you do the work, the results will be life-changing.

You might be wondering, "Who am I to guide you on this journey?" I'm not a guru or a self-proclaimed expert. I'm someone who's been where you are. I've faced my own inner saboteur, hit rock bottom, and clawed my way back up. Along the way, I've spent years studying psychology, neuroscience, and personal development, testing what works and what doesn't. This book is the culmination of that journey - a practical, no-nonsense guide to overcoming self-sabotage and unlocking your true potential.

So, are you ready to silence your inner saboteur and step into your power? Are you ready to stop holding yourself back and start living your most confident, capable life?

Great. Then, let's get started.

Turn the page, and take the first step on your transformation. The journey of a thousand miles begins with a single step. This is yours.

Let's walk this path together. Your new life is waiting.

Chapter One

The Surprising Truth About Your Inner Saboteur

The Surprising Upsides of Self-Defeat

We've all been there. That moment when you're about to do something amazing, something that could change your life for the better, and then... you don't. You back out. You make an excuse. You sabotage yourself.

It's frustrating, right? But what if I told you that this self-sabotage isn't all bad? What if, in some weird way, it's actually trying to help you?

Let's dive into this idea. It might just change how you see your inner saboteur.

First up, let's talk about comfort zones. We all have them. They're like our favorite old sweaters - maybe not the most stylish, but oh so cozy. When we self-sabotage, we're often just trying to stay in that cozy place.

Think about it. Change is scary. It's unknown. Our brains don't like the unknown - it could be dangerous! So when we're faced with a big change, even a good one, part of us goes, "Whoa, hold up! Let's stick with what we know."

This is your inner saboteur trying to keep you safe. It's not always right, but its heart (if saboteurs had hearts) is in the right place.

Next, let's consider disappointment. Nobody likes it. It's the vegetables of emotions - good for you, but not very tasty. When we self-sabotage, we're often trying to avoid a big helping of disappointment.

If you never try, you can never fail, right? It's a sneaky way our minds protect us from potential hurt.

It's like when you don't ask your crush out because "they probably don't like me anyway." You're protecting yourself from rejection. It's not the best strategy in the long run, but in the moment, it feels safer.

Lastly, there's control. We humans love feeling in control. It makes us feel safe and powerful. Self-sabotage can actually be a way of maintaining control.

If you're the one messing things up, at least you're the one in charge of the mess-up, right? It might sound weird, but sometimes it feels better to be in control of failure than to risk success that's out of our hands.

Let's look at a real-life example. Meet Sarah.

Sarah was stuck in a job she hated. She knew she could do better, but every time she landed a job interview, she'd find a reason to cancel at the last minute.

- She'd get "sick" the day of the interview.

- Her car would mysteriously break down.

- She'd decide she wasn't qualified after all and not show up.

This went on for months. Sarah was frustrated with herself. Why couldn't she just go to these interviews?

But here's the thing: Sarah's self-sabotage was actually trying to protect her.

You see, Sarah had been at her current job for ten years. It wasn't great, but she knew what to expect. She knew her coworkers, her boss, and her daily routine. It was comfortable.

The idea of a new job was exciting but also terrifying. What if her new coworkers didn't like her? What if the work was too hard? What if she failed?

By canceling these interviews, Sarah was:

1. Preserving her comfort zone

2. Avoiding potential disappointment

3. Maintaining a sense of control

Was it the best way to handle things? Probably not. But understanding why she was doing it was the first step to making a change.

Once Sarah realized what was happening, she was able to work on it. She started small, pushing herself out of her comfort zone in little ways. She spoke up more in meetings. She took on a new project at work.

As she got more comfortable with change and challenges, those job interviews started to seem less scary. She finally went to one, then another. And you know what? She got a great new job that she loves.

Sarah's story shows us that self-sabotage, while frustrating, isn't just random acts of self-destruction. It's often our mind's misguided attempt to protect us.

Understanding this can be a game-changer. Instead of beating yourself up over self-sabotage, you can get curious about it. What is it trying to protect you from? What fear is hiding behind it?

When you start seeing self-sabotage this way, you can work with it instead of against it. You can acknowledge the fear or discomfort, thank your inner saboteur for trying to help, and then gently push forward anyway.

It's like having a really overprotective friend. You appreciate that they care, but sometimes you need to tell them, "I got this."

So, next time you find yourself self-sabotaging, take a moment. Ask yourself:

- What am I afraid of?

- What am I trying to avoid?

- How am I trying to stay in control?

The answers might surprise you. And they might just be the key to moving past that self-sabotage and towards the things you really want.

Your inner saboteur isn't your enemy. It's just a part of you that's trying to help in its own clumsy way. By understanding it, you can start to work with it instead of against it.

And that's when the real magic happens. That's when you start to see self-sabotage not as a roadblock but as a signpost pointing you toward growth.

So here's to embracing our inner saboteurs, understanding their well-meaning but mis-guided efforts, and gently showing them a better way. Because when we do that, we open up a whole new world of possibilities.

After all, the surprising truth about your inner saboteur isn't just that it's trying to help. It's that when understood and redirected, it can become one of your greatest allies in personal growth and success.

And that's a truth worth exploring.

Echoes of Doubt from Our Ancestors

Let's take a journey back in time, way back. I'm talking about caveman days when our ancestors were just figuring out how not to get eaten by saber-toothed tigers. It might seem like we're worlds apart from those early humans, but guess what? We're not as different as you might think.

That little voice in your head that says, "Maybe I shouldn't?" It's not just you being a worry-wart. It's an echo from our past, a whisper from our ancestors saying, "Hey, be careful out there!"

Self-doubt isn't a modern problem we have picked up along with smartphones and avocado toast. It's an old, old friend that's been with us since the dawn of humanity. And believe it or not, it's been trying to keep us alive this whole time.

Let's break this down a bit.

First up, let's look at caution as a survival trait. Back in the day, being too bold could get you killed. Imagine you're a caveman (or cavewoman; let's not be sexist here). You see a nice, juicy fruit on a tree. Looks tasty, right? But wait - what if it's poisonous? What if a hungry predator is lurking nearby?

That moment of doubt, that hesitation, could save your life. The early humans who stopped to think, "Is this a good idea?" were more likely to survive and pass on their genes. And guess what? You're their descendant. You're the product of thousands of years of successful doubters!

Next, let's talk about group cohesion and social harmony. Humans are social creatures. We've always lived in groups, and getting along with others was crucial for survival.

Self-doubt played a big role here, too. It made us think twice before doing something that might upset the group. "Should I really take the last piece of mammoth meat? What if the others get mad at me?" This kind of thinking helped keep the peace and kept the group together.

In today's world, this shows up as things like, "Should I really speak up in this meeting? What if everyone thinks my idea is stupid?" It's not always helpful now, but it comes from a place of wanting to fit in and maintain social bonds.

Lastly, there's adaptation and learning from mistakes. Self-doubt gives us a chance to pause and reflect. It's like our brain's way of saying, "Hey, remember last time when we did this and it didn't go so well? Maybe we should try something different."

This ability to learn and adapt is what made humans so successful as a species. We didn't just charge ahead unthinkingly - we thought, we doubted, we reconsidered, and we improved.

Now, let's paint a picture of how this might have played out for our ancestors.

Imagine a small group of early humans. They're huddled around a fire as night falls, the sounds of unknown creatures echoing in the darkness. Among them is Grug, a young and eager hunter.

Grug has spotted tracks of a large animal nearby. He's excited - bringing down this beast could feed the whole tribe for days. He wants to go after it right away.

But then, that little voice of doubt kicks in. Grug hesitates. He remembers the last time someone went hunting at night. They never came back.

The doubt makes Grug pause. He looks around at his tribe, at the children sleeping peacefully, at the elders who rely on the younger members for protection. Is it worth risking leaving them vulnerable?

Grug decides to wait until morning. When the sun rises, he and a few other hunters follow the tracks. They find not one but a whole herd of animals. By working together in the daylight, they're able to bring down several, providing food for the tribe for weeks.

If Grug hadn't listened to that voice of doubt, things could have gone very differently. He might have been injured or killed hunting alone in the dark. The tribe would have lost a strong young hunter and maybe even faced hunger.

This is how self-doubt worked for our ancestors. It wasn't about holding them back - it was about helping them make smarter, safer choices.

Now, you might be thinking, "That's great for cavemen, but what about me? I'm not exactly fighting off saber-toothed tigers here."

And you're right. Our world is very different now. But our brains? They're still running a lot of that old software.

When you doubt yourself before a big presentation, that's your inner caveman worrying about being kicked out of the tribe. When you hesitate to try something new, that's your prehistoric brain trying to keep you safe from unknown dangers.

Understanding this can be a game-changer. It means your self-doubt isn't some personal flaw or weakness. It's an ancient survival tool that's just a bit confused by our modern world.

So next time that voice of doubt pipes up, try this:

- Take a deep breath and thank your inner caveman for trying to keep you safe.

- Ask yourself, "Is this doubt helping me, or is it an outdated response?"

- If it's not helpful, gently remind yourself that you're not in the Stone Age anymore.

It's about finding a balance. We don't want to ignore our instincts completely - sometimes, that voice of caution is right! But we also don't want to let an overeager survival instinct hold us back from the amazing things we can achieve in our modern world.

By understanding where our self-doubt comes from, we can start to work with it rather than against it. We can learn to recognize when it's being helpful and when it's just an echo from a time long past.

And that's the real power here. When you understand your self-doubt, you can start to use it as a tool rather than seeing it as an obstacle. You can let it inform your decisions without letting it control them.

So here's to our doubtful ancestors, who survived long enough to pass on their genes (and their worries) to us. And here's to us, learning to navigate this modern world with our stone-age brains.

Your self-doubt isn't your enemy. It's just an old friend trying to keep you safe in a world that doesn't exist anymore. Treat it with kindness, listen to it when it's helpful, and gently let it go when it's not.

After all, you're the result of millions of years of successful evolution. You've got this.

Self-Sabotage's Secret

Let's talk about self-sabotage. You know, that thing where you're about to do something great, and then. . . you don't. It's like you're your own worst enemy sometimes, right? But here's the kicker: what if your self-sabotage is actually trying to help you?

I know, I know. It sounds unbelievable. But stick with me here. We're about to uncover self-sabotage's secret, and it might just change how you see yourself.

First things first: self-sabotage isn't about you being lazy, dumb, or not good enough. It's about protection. Your brain is trying to keep you safe. It's just doing it in a really weird, backward way.

Let's break this down a bit.

Identifying the underlying fears

When you self-sabotage, there's always a fear hiding underneath. Maybe it's fear of failure, or fear of success (yep, that's a thing), or fear of change. Your job is to play detective and figure out what that fear is.

Think about the last time you self-sabotaged. Maybe you put off starting that big project until the last minute. Or you "forgot" to send that important email. What were you afraid might happen if you actually did the thing?

- Were you afraid you'd fail and look stupid?

- Were you afraid you'd succeed and then have to live up to higher expectations?

- Were you afraid things would change, and you wouldn't be able to handle it?

Once you know what you're afraid of, you can start to deal with it head-on.

Recognizing good intentions gone awry

Here's where it gets interesting. Your self-sabotage? It's actually trying to help. It's like a really overprotective friend who won't let you leave the house in case you stub your toe.

Your brain is saying, "Hey, if we don't try, we can't fail!" Or, "If we stay where we are, at least we know what to expect." It's trying to keep you safe and comfortable.

The problem is it's working with outdated information. Your brain doesn't know the difference between a saber-toothed tiger and a tough work presentation. It's just trying to avoid anything that seems scary or dangerous.

When you realize this, it changes everything. Instead of getting mad at yourself for self-sabotaging, you can start to feel a little compassion. Your brain is just trying its best to protect you.

Transforming self-sabotage into self-support

So how do we take this well-meaning but misguided self-sabotage and turn it into something helpful? That's where the magic happens.

Instead of fighting your self-sabotage, try talking to it. Sounds weird, I know, but bear with me. When you feel that urge to procrastinate or back out, pause for a moment. Ask yourself:

- What am I afraid of right now?

- What is my self-sabotage trying to protect me from?

- How can I address this fear more healthily?

By doing this, you're turning your self-sabotage into a tool for self-understanding. You're using it as a compass to point you toward the things you need to work on.

Let me tell you about my client, Angie. Angie was a brilliant writer who always dreamed of publishing a novel. But every time she sat down to write, she'd find a million other things to do instead. She'd clean her entire house, organize her sock drawer, and do anything but write.

Angie came to me feeling frustrated and angry with herself. "I'm just lazy," she told me. "I don't have what it takes to be a real writer."

But as we dug deeper, we discovered something interesting. Angie wasn't lazy at all. She was terrified.

You see, Angie had this fear that if she actually finished her novel, people might read it. And if people read it, they might not like it. And if they didn't like it, it would prove that Angie wasn't good enough.

So her brain, trying to protect her from this perceived threat, would come up with all sorts of ways to avoid writing. It was self-sabotage in action.

Once Angie understood this, everything changed. Instead of beating herself up for being "lazy," she started to approach her writing blocks with curiosity and compassion.

When she felt the urge to procrastinate, she'd pause and ask herself what she was afraid of. She'd acknowledge the fear, thank her brain for trying to protect her, and then gently redirect herself back to writing.

Angie also started to challenge her fears. She joined a writing group and shared her work, bit by bit. She discovered that even when people had critiques, it wasn't the end of the world. In fact, it often made her writing better.

Over time, Angie's self-sabotage transformed into self-support. That same instinct that used to hold her back now helped her identify areas where she needed to grow or heal.

And guess what? Angie finished her novel. It wasn't easy, and there were still moments of doubt and fear. However, by understanding her self-sabotage, she was able to work with it instead of against it.

So, what can we learn from Angie's story?

1. Self-sabotage often comes from a place of fear.

2. It's not about being lazy or not good enough; it's about protection.

3. By understanding the fear behind the sabotage, we can address it directly.

4. With time and practice, we can transform self-sabotage into a tool for growth.

This doesn't mean it's easy. Changing the way you think about yourself and your behaviors takes time and patience. But it's so worth it.

Imagine being able to look at your self-sabotaging behaviors with curiosity instead of judgment. Imagine being able to say, "I see you're trying to protect me. Thanks, but I've got this."

That's the power of understanding self-sabotage's secret. It's not your enemy. It's a misguided friend that, with a little guidance, can become your greatest ally.

So, the next time you find yourself procrastinating, backing out of an opportunity, or in any way sabotaging your success, take a moment. Breathe. And ask yourself:

- What am I afraid of?

- How is this behavior trying to protect me?

- How can I address this fear more healthily?

You might be surprised at what you discover. And that discovery? It's the first step towards turning your self-sabotage into your secret weapon for growth and success.

You're not broken. You're not lazy. You're just human with a brain that sometimes gets a little overprotective. And that's okay. With understanding and practice, you can learn to work with your brain instead of against it.

And that's when the real magic happens.

Unmasking the Saboteur Within

Let's talk about unmasking the saboteur within. You know, that sneaky part of you that seems to trip you up just when things are going well. It's like having a mischievous little gremlin living in your head, isn't it? But here's the thing - to deal with this saboteur, we first need to see it clearly. And that's where self-awareness comes in.

Self-awareness is like turning on the lights in a dark room. Suddenly, you can see all the stuff that was there all along but hidden in the shadows. It's not always comfortable, but boy, is it powerful.

Let's break this down into three key areas:

1. Mindfulness practices for identifying thought patterns

Mindfulness isn't just for yoga gurus and meditation masters. It's a practical tool that can help you catch your saboteur in the act.

Here's how it works: You start paying attention to your thoughts without judging them. It's like being a curious observer of your own mind.

Try this: Set aside 5 minutes each day to just sit quietly and notice your thoughts. Don't try to change them or push them away. Just watch them come and go like clouds in the sky.

Over time, you'll start to notice patterns. Maybe you always think, "I'm not good enough" before a big meeting. Or perhaps you tell yourself, "I'll never be able to do this," when faced with a new challenge. These are your saboteur's favorite lines, and now you can start to recognize them.

2. Journaling to track behaviors and triggers

Writing things down can be incredibly powerful. It's like creating a map of your inner world.

Start a journal. Each day, jot down:

- Any instances where you felt you might be sabotaging yourself

- What was happening at the time

- What you were thinking and feeling

Over time, you'll start to see patterns. Maybe you always procrastinate when you're feeling overwhelmed. Or perhaps you pick fights with your partner when you're feeling insecure about work.

This isn't about beating yourself up. It's about gathering information. The more you know about your saboteur's tactics, the better equipped you'll be to outsmart it.

3. Seeking feedback from trusted sources

Sometimes, it's hard to see ourselves clearly. That's where trusted friends, family, or colleagues can be invaluable.

Ask people you trust to give you honest feedback. What patterns do they notice in your behavior? When do they see you holding yourself back?

This isn't about criticism. It's about gaining a fuller picture of yourself. Sometimes, others can see things in us that we can't see ourselves.

Now, let me tell you about Alex. Alex was a talented marketing executive who always seemed to stumble just when a big opportunity came up. He'd freeze in important presentations or send emails with careless mistakes to key clients.

Alex came to me feeling frustrated and confused. "I know I'm good at my job," he said. "So why do I keep messing up?"

We started with a simple mindfulness practice. Every morning, Alex would spend 5 minutes just sitting quietly and observing his thoughts. At first, it felt awkward and pointless. But after a few weeks, Alex started to notice something interesting.

Whenever he thought about an upcoming presentation or important meeting, his mind would flood with thoughts like "You're going to mess this up" or "They're going to realize you're a fraud."

These thoughts had been there all along, but Alex had never really noticed them before. They were like background noise, constantly playing but just below his conscious awareness.

Next, we added journaling. Alex started writing down these thoughts when he noticed them, along with what was happening at the time. He also noted instances where he felt he'd sabotaged himself at work.

A pattern emerged. Alex realized that his self-sabotage often happened when he was about to step into a more visible role or take on more responsibility. His inner saboteur was trying to keep him "safe" by keeping him small.

Finally, Alex reached out to a few trusted colleagues for feedback. Their insights were eye-opening. They saw Alex as highly competent but noticed that he often downplayed his achievements or avoided taking credit for his successes.

Armed with this new self-awareness, Alex was able to start making changes. When he noticed those sabotaging thoughts creeping in, he could take a deep breath and remind himself that these were just old patterns, not facts.

He started practicing positive self-talk before big meetings. He'd remind himself of past successes and visualize things going well. It felt awkward at first, but over time, it became more natural.

Alex also started sharing his insights with his team. By being open about his struggles and efforts to overcome them, he created a culture of growth and self-improvement in his department.

The results were remarkable. Within six months, Alex had successfully led a major project and received a promotion. More importantly, he felt more confident and in control of his career.

So, what can we learn from Alex's story?

- Mindfulness can help us catch self-sabotaging thoughts in action

- Journaling can reveal patterns we might not otherwise notice

- Feedback from others can provide valuable insights we might miss on our own

- Self-awareness is the first step to making positive changes

Now, let's recap the key points we've covered:

1. Self-sabotage often serves as a misguided protection mechanism. It's not trying to hurt you – it's trying to keep you safe, just in a really unhelpful way.

2. Our tendency towards self-doubt has deep evolutionary roots. It's not a personal flaw – it's part of being human.

3. Reframing self-sabotage with compassion can lead to positive change. When we understand where it's coming from, we can work with it rather than against it.

4. Self-awareness is a powerful tool in overcoming self-sabotaging behaviors. The more we understand ourselves, the better equipped we are to make positive changes.

So, what now? Here are some action steps you can take:

1. Begin a daily mindfulness practice, even if just for 5 minutes. Remember, you're not trying to clear your mind - just observe your thoughts.

2. Start a journal to track instances of self-sabotage and potential triggers. Look for patterns over time.

3. Identify one self-sabotaging behavior and brainstorm three alternative responses. What could you do differently next time?

Remember, this is a journey. Be patient with yourself. Every step towards greater self-awareness is a step towards a more fulfilling, successful life.

Now that we've unmasked our inner saboteur, it's time to take things to the next level. In the next chapter, we'll explore how to turn that pesky inner critic into your biggest cheerleader. Get ready to transform negative self-talk into a powerful force for success!

Chapter Two

Turning Your Inner Critic into Your Biggest Fan

Unmask Your Inner Critic's Favorite Lines

W e all have that little voice inside our heads. You know the one I'm talking about. It's the voice that tells you you're not good enough, smart enough, or talented enough. It's your inner critic, and it's time we had a chat about it.

Let's face it: your inner critic can be a real jerk sometimes. But here's the thing: understanding how it talks to you is the first step in shutting it up. So, let's get started and unmask some of your inner critic's favorite lines.

Common negative self-talk patterns

Your inner critic has a few go-to phrases it loves to use. Here are some of the most common ones:

- "You're not good enough."

- "You're going to fail."

- "Everyone else is better than you."

- "You don't deserve success."

- "Who do you think you are?"

Sound familiar? These lines are like your inner critic's greatest hits album. They play on repeat in your head, wearing you down bit by bit.

But here's an important point: these thoughts aren't facts. They're just opinions - and pretty lousy ones at that. Your inner critic isn't some all-knowing guru. It's more like a grumpy old man yelling at clouds.

The impact of childhood experiences on your inner critic

Now, let's talk about where your inner critic comes from. Spoiler alert: it's not just magically appearing out of thin air.

Your childhood plays a big role in shaping your inner critic. Think back to when you were a kid. What messages did you hear about yourself? Maybe your parents always pushed you to get straight A's. Or maybe you had a teacher who told you that you'd never amount to anything.

These experiences stick with us. They become the building blocks for our inner critic. It's like your brain is taking notes, and later, it uses those notes to write the script for your inner critic.

For example, if you grew up hearing that you needed to be perfect all the time, your inner critic might sound something like this: "You made a mistake? You're such a failure. You'll never be good enough."

Ouch, right? But remember, just because your inner critic learned these lines a long time ago doesn't mean they're true.

How societal expectations shape your internal dialogue

It's not just your childhood that shapes your inner critic. Society has a big say in it, too. We're bombarded with messages about how we should look, act, and live our lives.

Social media doesn't help. It's like a highlight reel of everyone else's perfect lives. Your inner critic sees all this and goes into overdrive. "Look at her perfect job. Why can't you be that successful?" or "He's in such great shape. You're so lazy for not working out every day."

These societal expectations seep into our internal dialogue. They become the measuring stick our inner critic uses to judge us. And let me tell you, it's a pretty unfair measuring stick.

Michelle, a marketing executive, realizes her inner critic's voice mimics her perfectionist father's, affecting her confidence at work.

Let's talk about Michelle. She's a hotshot marketing executive, but she's always second-guessing herself at work. Her inner critic is constantly telling her she's not good enough, that her ideas are stupid, and that she's going to mess up big time.

One day, Michelle has a lightbulb moment. She realizes that her inner critic sounds suspiciously like her dad. Her dad was a total perfectionist when she was growing up. Nothing was ever good enough for him.

Michelle's childhood memories come flooding back. She remembers her dad criticizing her school projects, telling her she could do better even when she got A's. She recalls him nitpicking her cleaning skills when she helped around the house.

This realization hits Michelle like a ton of bricks. Her inner critic isn't her voice at all – it's her dad's! All those years, she'd been carrying around her dad's perfectionist standards in her head, letting them chip away at her confidence.

But here's where things get interesting. Once Michelle recognizes this, she starts to change how she talks to herself. When her inner critic pipes up with, "Your presentation is terrible. You're going to look like an idiot," Michelle pauses.

She takes a deep breath and thinks, "Wait a minute. That's not me talking. That's my dad's old perfectionist voice. I don't have to listen to it."

Michelle starts to challenge her inner critic. She asks herself, "Is this really true? Or is this just my old programming talking?" More often than not, she realizes it's the latter.

Over time, Michelle learns to recognize when her inner critic is mimicking her dad's voice. She starts to separate her own thoughts from these old, unhelpful patterns. It's not easy, and it doesn't happen overnight. Slowly, however, Michelle started to feel more confident at work.

She begins to trust her ideas more. She stops second-guessing every decision. And you know what? Her work actually improves. Without the constant criticism in her head, Michelle feels free to be creative and take risks.

Michelle's story shows us something important. Our inner critic often borrows its script from our past. But once we recognize this, we can start to rewrite that script.

So, what about you? Does your inner critic sound like someone from your past? Maybe a parent, a teacher, or a mean kid from school? Take a moment to listen to your inner critic. Really listen. You might be surprised at what you hear.

Recognizing the voice of your inner critic is the first step in taking away its power. It's like turning on the lights and realizing the monster in the closet was just a pile of clothes all along.

Your inner critic might be loud, but that doesn't mean it's right. It's just a collection of old thoughts and outdated beliefs. You have the power to challenge it, to question it, and ultimately, to change it.

So the next time your inner critic starts yapping, take a page from Michelle's book. Pause, take a breath, and ask yourself: "Is this really my voice? Or is it just old programming?"

You might just find that your inner critic isn't as scary - or as right - as you thought it was.

Taming Your Mind's Harshest Voice

Let's talk about that pesky voice in your head. You know, the one that's always ready with a snappy put-down or a dire prediction. It's your inner critic, and it's time we gave it a makeover.

Now, you might be thinking, "Why would I want to make friends with that jerk?" because we're about to uncover some surprising truths about your mind's harshest voice.

Understanding the protective intent behind criticism

Here's a plot twist for you: your inner critic isn't actually out to get you. I know, I know, it sure feels like it sometimes. But hear me out.

Your inner critic is like an overprotective parent. It's trying to keep you safe, but it's going about it all wrong. It thinks that if it points out every possible flaw or failure, you'll be prepared for anything. It's like a really bad life coach.

Think about it this way: if you were about to step out in front of a car, you'd want someone to yell at you to stop, right? Your inner critic is doing the same thing but for every little thing in your life. It's exhausting, but it means well.

So the next time your inner critic pipes up, try to remember: it's not trying to hurt you. It's just really, really bad at showing it cares.

Techniques for dialoguing with your inner critic

Okay, so now that we know your inner critic isn't the villain we thought it was, how do we talk to it? Here are some techniques to try:

1. Name it to tame it: Give your inner critic a name. It might sound silly, but it helps create some distance between you and those critical thoughts. Maybe your inner critic is "Debbie Downer" or "Negative Ned."

2. Thank it (yes, really): When your inner critic speaks up, try saying, "Thanks for your input." It acknowledges the concern without giving it power.

3. Ask for evidence: Challenge your inner critic. If it says, "You're going to fail," ask, "What proof do you have?" Often, there isn't any.

4. Reframe the criticism: Turn "You're not good enough" into "You have room to improve." It's a small shift, but it can make a big difference.

5. Imagine a dialogue: Picture sitting down with your inner critic for a chat. What would you say to it? What might it say back?

These techniques might feel weird at first. That's okay. You're learning a new language - the language of self-compassion. It takes practice, but it's worth it.

Harnessing your inner critic's energy for motivation

Now, here's where things get really interesting. What if I told you that your inner critic could actually be a source of motivation? It's true!

Your inner critic has a lot of energy. It's always on, always ready with a comment. Instead of trying to silence it completely (which, let's face it, is pretty much impossible), we can redirect that energy.

Here's how:

1. Use criticism as a challenge: When your inner critic says, "You can't do it," respond with "Watch me."

2. Turn put-downs into goals: If your inner critic says, "Your presentation skills suck," make improving your public speaking a goal.

3. Embrace the fear: If your inner critic is afraid of failure, use that fear to fuel your preparation.

4. Celebrate small wins: Every time you prove your inner critic wrong, even in small ways, celebrate it. This builds confidence over time.

The goal isn't to entirely get rid of your inner critic. It's to turn it from a screaming backseat driver into a slightly nervous but supportive co-pilot.

Narrative: James, an aspiring author, learns to view his inner critic as a well-intentioned editor, leading to improved writing and reduced anxiety.

Let's talk about James. He's always dreamed of being a writer, but every time he sits down to write, his inner critic goes into overdrive. "This is terrible," it says. "No one will ever want to read this. You're wasting your time."

For years, James believed these thoughts. He'd start writing, then give up in frustration. His novel remained unfinished, a constant source of guilt and disappointment.

Then, one day, James had an idea. What if he treated his inner critic like an editor instead of an enemy? He decided to give it a try.

The next time James sat down to write and heard that familiar critical voice, he paused. Instead of getting frustrated, he said, "Thanks for your input, Editor. What specifically don't you like about this?"

To his surprise, his inner critic had some concrete suggestions. "The dialogue sounds stiff," it said. "And the pacing in this scene is too slow."

James was shocked. These were actually helpful comments! He realized that his inner critic wasn't trying to stop him from writing - it was trying to help him write better.

From that day on, James started to view his inner critic differently. He imagined it as a well-intentioned but overzealous editor, always eager to point out areas for improvement.

When his inner critic said, "This chapter is boring," James would respond, "Okay, Editor, how can we make it more exciting?" He'd brainstorm ideas for plot twists or character development.

When his inner critic insisted, "No one will want to read this," James would ask, "What would make it more engaging for readers?" This led him to think more deeply about his target audience and what they might enjoy.

Over time, James noticed something amazing happening. His writing was actually improving. By treating his inner critic as a collaborator rather than an enemy, he was able to use its input constructively.

But that wasn't the only change. James found that he was enjoying writing more than ever before. The constant anxiety and self-doubt that used to plague him had diminished. He still heard his inner critic, but now it felt more like a writing partner than a harsh judge.

James finished his novel. It wasn't perfect - no first draft ever is - but he was proud of it. And when it came time to do revisions, he found he was actually looking forward to working with his "inner editor."

James's story shows us something important. Our inner critic doesn't have to be our enemy. With a little reframing, it can become a valuable ally in our personal growth.

So, what's the takeaway here? Your inner critic isn't going anywhere. It's a part of you. But you get to decide what kind of part it plays. Is it the villain in your story, always trying to bring you down? Or is it a well-meaning (if sometimes misguided) helper pushing you to be your best?

The choice is yours. You have the power to change your relationship with your inner critic. It might take time, and it definitely takes practice. But the payoff - increased confidence, reduced anxiety, and maybe even better work - is worth it.

Remember, your inner critic is just trying to help. It's not very good at it, but hey, it's trying. So the next time you hear that critical voice in your head, take a deep breath and say, "Thanks for your input. Now, how can we make this better?"

You might be surprised at the conversation that follows.

Your Feedback Transformation Toolkit

Alright, let's explore your Feedback Transformation Toolkit. This is where we get our hands dirty and really start to shake things up with your inner critic. Think of it as giving that pesky voice in your head a makeover. We're not trying to silence it completely - we're just teaching it some manners.

The "Criticism Reframe" technique

First up, we've got the "Criticism Reframe" technique. It's like putting on a pair of glasses that turns your inner critic's harsh words into useful feedback. Here's how it works:

1. Catch the criticism: When you hear that familiar critical voice, stop and listen.

2. Write it down: Jot down exactly what your inner critic is saying. Don't sugar-coat it.

3. Look for the concern: Ask yourself, "What's the worry behind this criticism?" Your inner critic might be saying, "You're going to mess up this presentation," but the real concern could be, "I want you to do well."

4. Reframe it: Now, turn that criticism into constructive feedback. "You're going to mess up" becomes "I want to make sure I'm well-prepared."

5. Make an action plan: Based on your reframe, what can you do? In this case, you might decide to practice your presentation more.

This technique takes practice, but it's like learning a new language. At first, it feels awkward and slow. But keep at it, and soon, you'll be fluent in turning criticism into fuel for growth.

Journaling exercises for self-reflection and positive self-talk

Now, let's talk about journaling. I know, I know, it might sound a bit cheesy. But stick with me here. Journaling is like a gym for your mind. It helps you build those positive self-talk muscles. Here are some exercises to try:

1. The Daily Win: Every day, write down one thing you did well. It doesn't have to be huge. Maybe you made a great sandwich or sent that email you've been putting off.

2. The Criticism Flip: When you catch yourself being self-critical, write it down. Then, flip it into a positive statement. "I'm so lazy" becomes "I'm taking time to rest and recharge."

3. The Future You Letter: Write a letter from your future self five years from now. What would they say about your current struggles? How would they encourage you?

4. The Gratitude Three: List three things you're grateful for about yourself. Maybe it's your sense of humor, your kindness, or even just your ability to make it through tough days.

5. The Inner Critic Dialogue: Have a written conversation with your inner critic. Ask it why it's so harsh. You might be surprised at what comes out.

Journaling isn't about perfect writing. It's about getting your thoughts out of your head and onto paper where you can look at them more objectively.

Visualization methods to amplify your inner cheerleader

Now, let's talk about visualization. It's not just for athletes and meditation gurus. You can use it to boost your inner cheerleader, too. Here's how:

1. The Supportive Friend: Close your eyes and imagine a friend who believes in you completely. What would they say about your abilities? How would they encourage you?

2. The Success Scene: Visualize yourself succeeding at something you're worried about. See it in vivid detail. How do you feel? What does success look like?

3. The Inner Critic Makeover: Picture your inner critic. Now, imagine giving it a makeover. Change its voice to something less threatening. Maybe give it a silly hat. Make it harder to take seriously.

4. The Confidence Power-Up: Imagine confidence as a glowing light. See it filling your body, making you stand taller and feel stronger.

5. The Future Highlight Reel: Visualize a "movie" of your future successes. See yourself overcoming challenges and achieving your goals.

These visualization exercises might feel a bit weird at first. That's okay. Your brain is learning a new skill. Keep practicing, and it'll start to feel more natural.

Anecdote: A group therapy session where participants role-play their inner critics, leading to breakthroughs in self-understanding.

Let me tell you about something wild that happened in a group therapy session I once observed. The therapist had this idea to have everyone role-play their inner critics. It sounded kind of goofy, but boy, did it lead to some eye-opening moments.

There was this one guy, let's call him Mike. Mike was always putting himself down, saying he wasn't smart enough or good enough. When it was his turn to play his inner critic, he stood up, puffed out his chest, and started speaking in this booming voice.

"You'll never amount to anything," he said, wagging his finger at an imaginary version of himself. "You're not as smart as your brother. You're lazy. You should just give up now."

The room got really quiet. Mike's face was red, and you could see he was fighting back tears. But then something amazing happened.

Another group member, Stacy, stood up. "Hey, Mike's inner critic," she said, "What's your problem? Why are you being so mean?"

Mike, still in character as his inner critic, looked surprised. "I'm just trying to protect him," he said. "If he doesn't try, he can't fail, right?"

And just like that, the floodgates opened. Mike realized his inner critic, as harsh as it was, was actually trying to shield him from disappointment. It was going about it all wrong, but its intentions weren't malicious.

As the session went on, more people took turns playing their inner critics. Some were funny, some were sad, but all of them were eye-opening. People started to see their inner critics not as enemies but as misguided protectors.

By the end of the session, the energy in the room had completely shifted. People were laughing, sharing strategies for talking back to their inner critics, and even giving their critics silly names to take away some of their power.

Mike left that day with a new understanding of his inner critic. He still heard that critical voice, but now he could say, "I know you're trying to protect me, but I've got this. Thanks for your concern, but I'm going to try anyway."

This story shows us something important. Our inner critics aren't these all-powerful, all-knowing voices. They're just parts of ourselves, often stuck in old patterns or fears. When we can see them for what they are, we can start to change our relationship with them.

So, what's the takeaway from all this? Your inner critic isn't the enemy. It's more like a misguided friend who needs some gentle redirection. With these tools - the Criticism Reframe, journaling exercises, visualization methods, and even a bit of role-play - you can start to transform your inner critic from a harsh judge into a supportive coach.

Remember, this is a process. It takes time and practice. There will be days when your inner critic seems louder than ever. That's okay. Just keep using these tools, keep practicing, and over time, you'll notice a shift.

Your inner critic isn't going away. But with these strategies, you can turn down its volume and turn up the volume on your inner cheerleader. And trust me, that cheerleader has been waiting a long time to be heard.

So, are you ready to start your feedback transformation? Your toolkit is right here. All you need to do is pick up the first tool and get to work. Your inner critic won't know what hit it.

Allies for Your Inner Cheerleader

Let's talk about building your cheerleading squad. No, I'm not suggesting you go out and buy pom-poms (unless that's your thing). We're talking about surrounding yourself with people who'll boost your confidence and help drown out that pesky inner critic.

Identifying and nurturing supportive relationships

First things first, let's figure out who's in your corner. Think about the people in your life. Who makes you feel good about yourself? Who believes in you, even when you don't believe in yourself? These are your potential allies.

Now, here's the tricky part: sometimes, the people closest to us aren't always the most supportive. Maybe your best friend is going through a tough time and can't be there for you. Or maybe your partner doesn't quite get your dreams. That's okay. We're not looking for perfection here.

Make a list of people who lift you up. It could be family, coworkers, or even that barista who always remembers your order and asks about your day. These are your potential cheerleaders.

Once you've identified these people, it's time to nurture these relationships. Here's how:

1. Be honest: Let them know you're working on your self-confidence. Most people want to help if they know how.

2. Show appreciation: Thank them when they support you. It reinforces the positive behavior.

3. Reciprocate: Be there for them too. Supportive relationships are a two-way street.

4. Set boundaries: If someone's support feels more like pressure, it's okay to take a step back.

Creating a "success team" of mentors and peers

Now, let's take it up a notch. We're going to create your very own "success team." This is like your personal board of directors but way less stuffy.

Your success team should include the following:

1. A mentor: Someone who's been where you want to go. They can offer guidance and perspective.

2. A peer: Someone at your level who's working towards similar goals. You can motivate each other and share experiences.

3. A cheerleader: Someone who believes in you unconditionally. They're there to boost your spirits when things get tough.

4. An accountability partner: Someone who'll check in on your progress and give you a gentle nudge when needed.

5. A devil's advocate: Someone who'll challenge your ideas (constructively). They help you think critically and prepare for obstacles.

Your success team doesn't have to be formal. You don't need to have meetings or anything (unless you want to). It's just about identifying these roles in your life and leaning on them when you need to.

Using affirmations and positive feedback loops

Okay, let's talk about affirmations. I know, I know, it might sound a bit cheesy. But hear me out. Affirmations are like vitamins for your self-esteem. They might not taste great at first, but they're good for you.

Here's how to create affirmations that actually work:

1. Make them specific: Instead of "I'm awesome," try "I'm great at solving problems."

2. Use present tense: Say "I am," not "I will be."

3. Keep them realistic: "I'm learning to speak in public with confidence" is better than "I'm the world's best public speaker."

4. Say them out loud: It feels weird, but it's more powerful than just thinking about them.

Now, let's create some positive feedback loops. This is where you set yourself up for success and then celebrate that success. Here's how:

1. Set small, achievable goals.

2. Tell your success team about these goals.

3. Achieve the goal (because it's small and achievable, remember?)

4. Celebrate with your success team.

5. Use that success to fuel your next goal.

It's like a snowball of success. Each win makes you more confident for the next challenge.

Emily, a shy college student, forms a study group that boosts her academic confidence and social skills.

Let me tell you about Emily. She was a first-year college student, smart as a whip but shy as can be. Her inner critic was always telling her she wasn't smart enough, that she didn't belong in college.

One day, in her Psychology 101 class, the professor suggested forming study groups. Emily's inner critic went into overdrive. "No one will want to study with you," it said. "You'll just slow them down."

But Emily decided to try something different. She took a deep breath and turned to the girl next to her. "Would you like to form a study group?" she asked, her voice barely above a whisper.

To her surprise, the girl, Sandy, smiled and said yes. They found two other students who wanted to join, and just like that, Emily had a study group.

At first, Emily was quiet in the group sessions. But as they met week after week, something started to change. Emily realized she knew more than she thought. When she explained concepts to her groupmates, they actually understood better.

Sandy noticed Emily's knack for explaining tough ideas. "You should be a teacher," she said one day. Emily blushed, but inside, she felt a spark of pride.

As the semester went on, Emily's confidence grew. She started speaking up more in class. She even raised her hand to answer questions sometimes. Her grades improved, too.

However, the biggest change was in how Emily saw herself. Her inner critic was still there, but now she had other voices to listen to. The voice of Sandy saying she'd be a great teacher. The voice of her study group thanking her for her help. The voice of her professor praising her insights in class.

By the end of the semester, Emily wasn't just doing better academically. She had made friends, improved her social skills, and discovered strengths she never knew she had.

Emily's story shows us the power of surrounding ourselves with supportive people. Her study group became her success team, helping her overcome her inner critic and discover her potential.

Recap of Key Points

Alright, let's do a quick recap:

- Recognizing your inner critic's voice is the first step to change. You can't fix what you don't acknowledge.

- Befriending your inner critic can transform self-doubt into motivation. It's not about silencing that voice but about changing its tone.

- Practical exercises can help reframe negative self-talk into constructive feedback. It takes practice, but it's worth it.

- Building a support system reinforces positive internal dialogue. You don't have to do this alone.

Action Steps

Ready to put this into action? Here's what you can do:

1. Keep a "critic journal" for one week, noting negative self-talk patterns. This will help you identify what your inner critic likes to harp on.

2. Practice the "Criticism Reframe" technique daily. Turn that criticism into constructive feedback.

3. Identify one supportive person with whom to share your goals and progress. Let them be your cheerleader.

4. Create three personalized affirmations to counter your most common criticisms. Make them specific and realistic.

You've done great work in this chapter. You've learned to recognize your inner critic, befriend it, and even start turning it into an ally. You've built a support system to reinforce your new, positive self-talk. But this is just the beginning.

You've changed the voices in your head. Now, it's time to change your actions in the world. Are you ready? Let's go!

Chapter Three

The Procrastination Paradox: Why Delay Can Be Your Secret Weapon

Unmasking Procrastination's Mental Maze

We've all been there. You sit down to start that big project, and suddenly, your brain decides it's the perfect time to alphabetize your spice rack or deep-clean the bathroom grout. Welcome to the wild world of procrastination!

But remember, procrastination isn't just about being lazy or disorganized. It's a complex mental maze with twists and turns that can leave even the most motivated person spinning in circles. Let's dive into this maze and see if we can find our way out together.

Fear: The Monster Under the Bed

Remember when you were a kid, and you were convinced there was a monster under your bed? But for grown-ups, the monster isn't real, even though the fear sure feels like it is.

When we procrastinate, we're often running from something scary. Maybe it's:

- Fear of failure

- Fear of success (yep, that's a thing!)

- Fear of criticism

- Fear of the unknown

These fears can make us doubt ourselves big time. We start thinking things like:

"What if I'm not good enough?"

"What if everyone hates my work?"

"What if I succeed and can't handle it?"

It's like our brains are throwing a doubt party, and we're the reluctant guests of honor.

Perfectionism: The Never-Ending Obstacle Course

Now, let's talk about perfectionism. It's like procrastination's annoying sidekick.

Perfectionism tricks us into thinking that if we can't do something perfectly, we shouldn't do it at all. It's like setting up an impossible obstacle course in our minds.

Here's how it messes with our confidence:

1. We set unrealistic standards for ourselves.

2. We focus on our flaws instead of our strengths.

3. We compare our behind-the-scenes to everyone else's highlight reel.

The result? We feel like we're never quite good enough, so we keep putting things off until we can do them "perfectly" (spoiler alert: that day never comes).

The Time Travel Tangle

Okay, here's where things get a bit sci-fi. One of the weirdest things about procrastination is how it messes with our sense of time. It's like our present self and our future self are in different time zones, and they're not communicating well.

When we procrastinate, we're essentially saying, "Future Me can handle this." But here's the problem: Future You is still you, just with less time and more stress. It's like we're playing a cruel game of hot potato with our tasks, tossing them to a future version of ourselves who we imagine will be magically more capable.

This disconnect can really mess with our confidence. We start to doubt our ability to follow through on things, which makes us even more likely to procrastinate in the future. It's a vicious cycle that can leave us feeling pretty crummy about ourselves.

Tammy's Story: From Procrastination to Publication

Let's take a break from all this theory and meet Tammy. Tammy's a super-talented writer who'd been working on her novel for years. The problem? She kept finding reasons not to finish it.

First, it was "I need to do more research." Then it was, "The first chapter isn't perfect yet." And finally, "What if everyone hates it?"

Sound familiar? Tammy was caught in the procrastination maze, trapped by fear, perfectionism, and a disconnect from her future self.

But here's where things get interesting. Tammy started to look at her procrastination differently. Instead of beating herself up about it, she got curious. She asked herself:

- What am I really afraid of?

- What would "good enough" look like for this project?

- How would Future Tammy feel if I finished this book?

As she dug into these questions, Tammy realized something pretty cool. Her procrastination wasn't just about avoiding work – it was her subconscious way of refining her ideas and building her confidence.

She started to see her "research rabbit holes" as ways to add depth to her story. Her obsession with perfecting the first chapter? That was her honing her writing skills. Even her fear of rejection pushed her to make her story the best it could be.

Tammy didn't overcome her procrastination overnight. But by reframing it as a tool rather than a flaw, she changed her relationship with it. She set small, manageable goals for her writing and celebrated each milestone.

And you know what? Six months later, Tammy finished her novel. It wasn't perfect (because nothing ever is), but it was done. And she was proud of it.

The Procrastination Reframe

So, what can we learn from Tammy's story? Procrastination isn't always the enemy. Sometimes, it's just our brain's weird way of trying to protect us or improve our work.

Here's how we can start to reframe procrastination:

1. Get curious about your procrastination. What's really behind it?

2. Look for the hidden benefits. Is your procrastination helping you in some way?

3. Set smaller, less scary goals. Big tasks are overwhelming. Tiny tasks are doable.

4. Celebrate your progress, no matter how small.

5. Remember that done is better than perfect.

Procrastination doesn't have to be a confidence killer. By understanding its roots in fear, perfectionism, and our relationship with our future selves, we can start to navigate the maze. And who knows? We might even find some treasure along the way.

Everyone procrastinates sometimes. It doesn't make you lazy or incapable. It just makes you human. So the next time you find yourself alphabetizing your sock drawer, instead of tackling that big project, take a deep breath. You're not avoiding work; you're just taking the scenic route to success.

The Unexpected Productivity Boost

Let's look at the wild world of procrastination's unexpected sidekick: productivity. Yep, you read that right. Sometimes, putting things off can actually make you more productive. Crazy, huh?

The Procrastination-Productivity Paradox

We've all been there. It's 11 PM, the night before a big deadline, and suddenly, your brain kicks into overdrive. Ideas are flowing, your fingers are flying across the keyboard, and you're wondering, "Where was this energy three weeks ago?"

Welcome to the world of "productive procrastination." It's like your brain's secret superpower that only activates when you're down to the wire. But why does this happen?

- Pressure cooker effect: Deadlines create urgency, which can boost focus and creativity.

- No time for perfectionism: When you're racing against the clock, you don't have time to obsess over every little detail.

- Adrenaline rush: The stress of an approaching deadline can give you a natural energy boost.

It's like your brain is a kid who won't clean their room until you threaten to take away their video games. Suddenly, they're a cleaning machine!

The Magic of Productive Procrastination

Now, don't get me wrong. I'm not saying you should always wait until the last minute to do everything. But there's something to be said for the creativity that can come from a little time pressure.

Here's how productive procrastination can work in your favor:

1. Incubation time: While you're "procrastinating," your brain is actually working on the problem in the background.

2. Fresh perspective: When you finally sit down to work, you might see the task with fresh eyes.

3. Efficiency boost: With limited time, you're forced to focus on what's truly important.

It's like your brain is a pressure cooker, and procrastination is turning up the heat. When you finally lift the lid, boom! Out comes a fully cooked idea.

Creating Your Own Deadlines

But what if you don't have a real deadline breathing down your neck? Good news! You can trick your brain into thinking you do.

Here are some ways to create artificial deadlines:

- Set a timer: Give yourself a specific amount of time to complete a task.

- Use a productivity app: Many apps simulate deadlines and add a fun, game-like element to your work.

- Make a public commitment: Tell someone you'll have something done by a certain time.

- Reward yourself: Promise yourself a treat if you finish by your self-imposed deadline.

It's like setting up your own mini-Olympics. Ready, set, procrastinate productively!

The Procrastination-Preparation Balance

Now, before you go canceling all your plans and waiting until the last minute for everything, let's talk balance. The key is to find the sweet spot between procrastination and preparation.

Here's how to strike that balance:

1. Do the groundwork early: Research, gather materials, and outline your ideas.

2. Let it simmer: Give your brain some time to process the information.

3. Set a "start" deadline: Decide when you'll begin the main work, leaving enough time for unexpected hiccups.

4. Work in focused bursts: Use techniques like the Pomodoro method to maintain productivity.

It's like cooking a gourmet meal. You prep the ingredients ahead of time, let the flavors marinate, and then bring it all together in a final burst of culinary creativity.

Alex's Procrastination Revelation

Meet Alex, a marketing executive with a knack for last-minute brilliance. His best campaigns always seemed to come together right before the deadline, leaving his team both impressed and stressed.

Alex noticed this pattern and decided to dig deeper. He realized that the pressure of a looming deadline kicked his creativity into high gear. But he also knew that constantly working under that kind of stress wasn't sustainable.

So, Alex got clever. He started creating his own "fake" deadlines:

- He'd tell his team the client wanted ideas two days earlier than the actual deadline.

- He'd schedule brainstorming sessions close to (but not too close to) the real due date.

- He'd break big projects into smaller chunks with their own mini-deadlines.

The result? Alex found a way to harness his procrastination superpowers without the panic of a real last-minute rush. His campaigns were still brilliant, but now he had time to refine and polish them before the actual deadline.

But here's the real kicker: Alex started applying this technique to other areas of his life. He'd give himself a "deadline" to start planning his vacation or to begin a home improvement project. Suddenly, areas of his life that had been stuck in perpetual procrastination started moving forward.

Procrastination: Your Secret Productivity Weapon

So, what can we learn from Alex's story and all this talk about productive procrastination? Here are the key takeaways:

1. Procrastination isn't always the enemy. Sometimes, it's just your brain's way of building up creative pressure.

2. You can create your own "productive procrastination" scenarios by setting artificial deadlines.

3. Balance is key. Do some prep work early, but leave room for that last-minute creative burst.

4. Pay attention to when you do your best work. If it's under pressure, find ways to recreate that pressure without the stress.

5. Don't beat yourself up for procrastinating. Instead, get curious about how you can use it to your advantage.

Procrastination is like spice in cooking. A little bit can add flavor to your productivity, but too much can ruin the whole dish. The trick is finding the right amount for your personal taste.

So, the next time you find yourself procrastinating, don't panic. Maybe you're not avoiding work – maybe you're just charging up your productivity superpowers. Just make sure you leave yourself enough time to actually use those powers before the real deadline hits!

And who knows? Maybe embracing your inner procrastinator (in moderation, of course) could be the key to unlocking your most creative, productive self. Now, that's a plot twist worthy of a procrastinator's last-minute brilliance!

Turning Delay into Action

Alright, let's talk about turning procrastination from your worst enemy into your secret weapon. Sounds impossible, right? Because we're about to flip the script on delay and turn it into a superpower for getting things done.

The Two-Minute Takeoff

Ever feel like starting a task is like trying to push a boulder uphill? You're not alone. That initial resistance can be a real productivity killer. But here's a neat trick: the "two-minute rule."

Here's how it works:

1. If a task takes less than two minutes, do it right away.

2. For bigger tasks, just commit to working on it for two minutes.

It's like dipping your toe in the water instead of cannonballing into the deep end. Often, once you start, you'll find yourself sailing past that two-minute mark without even noticing.

Why does this work? It's all about momentum. Starting is usually the hardest part. Once you're moving, it's easier to keep going. It's like pushing a car - it takes a lot of effort to get it rolling, but once it's moving, it's much easier to keep it going.

So, next time you're procrastinating, try the two-minute rule. You might be surprised at how often those two minutes turn into twenty or two hundred!

The Procrastination Incubation Station

Now, let's talk about something really cool: using your procrastination time as an idea incubator. It's like turning your brain into a slow cooker for creativity.

When you're avoiding a task, your brain doesn't just shut off. It's actually working on the problem in the background, kind of like a computer running a program in the background while you're doing other things.

Here's how to make the most of this "incubation time":

- Expose yourself to different stimuli: Read books, watch documentaries, go for a walk. You never know what might spark an idea.

- Let your mind wander: Daydreaming isn't just goofing off - it's giving your brain space to make new connections.

- Keep a notebook handy: When ideas pop up (and they will), jot them down.

It's like planting seeds in a garden. You might not see anything happening on the surface, but underneath, those ideas are taking root and growing.

Structured Procrastination: The Productivity Paradox

Now, here's where things get really interesting: structured procrastination. It sounds like an oxymoron, right? But stick with me here.

The idea is to use your tendency to procrastinate on one task to get a bunch of other stuff done. Here's how it works:

1. Make a to-do list with your most important (and probably most daunting) task at the top.

2. Fill the rest of the list with other tasks that need doing.

3. When you find yourself avoiding that top task, tackle the other items on your list instead.

It's like tricking your brain into being productive. You're still technically procrastinating on your main task, but you're getting a ton of other stuff done in the process.

The result? You end up being super productive, even while you're "procrastinating." It's like cleaning your entire house to avoid doing your taxes; your house gets clean, and eventually, you'll get to those taxes, too.

Maria's Procrastination Transformation

Let's meet Maria, a software developer who used to beat herself up for procrastinating. She'd sit at her computer, knowing she should be coding, but instead find herself scrolling through social media or reorganizing her desk for the millionth time.

But then Maria had an aha moment. She realized that during these "procrastination periods," her mind was actually chewing on coding problems in the background. So, instead of fighting her procrastination, she decided to work with it.

Here's what Maria did:

1. She started keeping a notebook next to her computer. Whenever she had an idea during her procrastination time, she'd jot it down.

2. She began using the two-minute rule. If she was stuck, she'd tell herself, "Just write one line of code." Often, that one line would turn into many more.

3. She embraced structured procrastination. When she didn't feel like tackling her main coding task, she'd work on documentation or answer colleague questions instead.

The results were amazing. Maria found that when she did sit down to code, she was more efficient and creative. Those ideas she jotted down during her "procrastination" often turned into innovative solutions. Thanks to structured procrastination, other aspects of her work improved, too.

Maria didn't eliminate procrastination - she transformed it into a powerful tool for problem-solving and productivity.

Turning Delay into Your Secret Weapon

So, what can we learn from all this? Procrastination doesn't have to be the productivity killer we often think it is. With the right approach, it can actually boost your creativity and efficiency. Here's how to make procrastination work for you:

1. Use the two-minute rule to overcome initial resistance. Sometimes, all you need is to start.

2. Embrace "productive procrastination" by using delay time for idea incubation. Let your mind wander - it might stumble onto something brilliant.

3. Try structured procrastination. Use your tendency to avoid one task as motivation to complete others.

4. Pay attention to your procrastination patterns. When do you procrastinate? What do you do instead? There might be valuable insights hidden in those habits.

5. Be kind to yourself. Procrastination is normal. Instead of beating yourself up, get curious about how you can use it to your advantage.

The goal isn't to eliminate procrastination entirely. That's like trying to stop the tide - it's just not going to happen. Instead, we're aiming to transform procrastination from a stumbling block into a stepping stone.

So, the next time you find yourself procrastinating, don't panic. Take a deep breath and ask yourself: "How can I use this delay to my advantage?" Maybe you'll brainstorm a brilliant idea. Maybe you'll knock out a bunch of small tasks you've been putting off. Or maybe you'll just give your brain the break it needs to come back to your main task refreshed and ready to go.

Procrastination doesn't have to be your enemy. With a little reframing and some clever strategies, it might just become your secret weapon for success.

Rewrite Your Procrastination Story

Let's get right into the fascinating world of rewriting your procrastination story. Buckle up because we're about to flip the script on how you think about putting things off!

The Power of Your Inner Dialogue

You know that little voice in your head? The one that whispers (or sometimes shouts) things like "You're so lazy!" or "Why can't you just get started?" That's your inner narrator, and it's time for a serious rewrite.

The way we talk to ourselves about procrastination can make a huge difference in how we feel and perform. It's like being the star of your own movie; you get to choose whether it's a tragedy or a triumph.

Catching Those Sneaky Self-Critical Thoughts

First things first, we need to become aware of those self-critical thoughts. They can be sneaky, popping up so quickly we hardly notice them. But they pack a punch, undermining our confidence and increasing our stress.

Common procrastination-related thoughts include:

- "I'm just lazy."

- "I always leave things to the last minute."

- "I can't work well under pressure."

Sound familiar? Don't worry, you're not alone. These thoughts are super common. But here's the thing: just because you think something doesn't mean it's true.

Challenge Those Thoughts!

Once you've caught those pesky self-critical thoughts, it's time to challenge them. It's like being a detective in your own mind, questioning the evidence and looking for alternative explanations.

For example:

- Instead of "I'm just lazy," try "I might be avoiding this task for a reason. What am I afraid of?"

- Replace "I always leave things to the last minute" with "I often work well under pressure. How can I use this to my advantage?"

- Swap "I can't work well under pressure" for "I've successfully completed tasks under pressure before. I can do it again."

It's not about positive thinking or denying reality. It's about being fair and balanced in how you interpret your behavior.

Embracing Your Pressure Superpowers

Now, here's where things get really interesting. What if, instead of seeing your tendency to work under pressure as a flaw, you saw it as a superpower?

Many people find they're more creative, focused, and efficient when working under a bit of pressure. It's like your brain kicks into overdrive, and suddenly, you're capable of amazing things.

Try thinking:

- "I thrive under pressure. It brings out my best work."

- "Last-minute inspiration often leads to my most creative ideas."

- "I'm adaptable and can produce quality work in short timeframes."

These aren't just empty affirmations. They're recognizing real strengths that many procrastinators have.

Positive Affirmations: Your New Procrastination Playlist

Speaking of affirmations, let's talk about how to use them to reframe procrastination. Think of these as your new theme song, playing in the background as you tackle your tasks.

Some powerful affirmations might be:

- "My ability to work under pressure is a valuable skill."

- "I trust in my capacity to complete tasks efficiently when needed."

- "Delaying tasks sometimes allows my ideas to fully develop."

Repeat these to yourself regularly, especially when you're feeling stressed about procrastination. It's like reprogramming your brain to see procrastination in a new light.

Tom's Transformation: From Panic to Performance

Meet Tom, a college student who always left studying to the last minute. He'd beat himself up about it, thinking he was lazy and undisciplined. As exams approached, his anxiety would skyrocket, making it even harder to focus.

But then Tom learned about reframing his procrastination story. He started to challenge his self-critical thoughts and embrace his ability to work under pressure.

Here's what Tom did:

1. He caught himself thinking, "I'm so lazy," and replaced it with "I work best under a bit of pressure."

2. He started seeing his last-minute studying as a strength, focusing on how it helped him retain information better.

3. He used affirmations like "I trust in my ability to prepare effectively in a short time."

The result? Tom's exam anxiety decreased significantly. He felt more confident going into tests, knowing he had a track record of performing well under pressure. And here's the proof - his grades actually improved!

Tom didn't completely stop procrastinating. But by changing his story about it, he reduced his stress and boosted his performance.

Rewriting Your Procrastination Story: A Recap

So, what have we learned about rewriting our procrastination story?

1. Our inner dialogue about procrastination can significantly impact our stress levels and performance.

2. Catching and challenging self-critical thoughts is key to changing our procrastination narrative.

3. Recognizing the potential benefits of working under pressure can turn procrastination from a weakness into a strength.

4. Positive affirmations can help reinforce a more empowering view of our work habits.

The goal isn't to eliminate procrastination. It's about changing how you think and feel about it, reducing stress, and boosting confidence in the process.

Action Steps: Your Procrastination Rewrite Toolkit

Ready to start rewriting your own procrastination story? Here are some concrete steps you can take:

1. Keep a thought journal for a week. Write down your self-critical thoughts about procrastination as you notice them.

2. For each negative thought, write down a more balanced or positive alternative.

3. List three times when working under pressure led to a good outcome for you.

4. Write your own set of positive affirmations about your ability to work effectively, even when you've delayed starting.

5. Practice saying these affirmations to yourself daily, especially when you're feeling stressed about a looming deadline.

Remember, changing your inner dialogue takes time and practice. Be patient with yourself. You're not just changing a habit - you're rewriting a story you've been telling yourself for years.

As we wrap up this chapter on the procrastination paradox, we've uncovered some surprising truths. We've seen how delay can sometimes be a secret weapon, how last-minute pressure can spark creativity, and how changing our internal narrative can transform our relationship with procrastination.

Chapter Four

Failure as Your North Star: Navigating Towards Success

The Hidden Path to Success

We've all been there. That sinking feeling in your stomach when things don't go as planned. The voice in your head that whispers, "You're not good enough." The urge to give up and throw in the towel. But what if I told you that these moments of failure are actually your secret weapon?

Yep, you heard that right. Failure isn't the bad guy we've made it out to be. It's more like a misunderstood friend who's trying to help us out. Let's delve into why failure might just be your ticket to success.

Embrace failure as feedback, not finality

Think of failure as a GPS recalculating your route. It's not telling you to give up on your destination; it's just helping you find a better way to get there.

When we fail, our first instinct is often to beat ourselves up. But here's a wild idea: What if we thanked our failures instead? Seriously, give it a shot. Next time something doesn't work out, try saying, "Thanks for the lesson, failure!" out loud. You might feel a bit silly, but it can really shift your perspective.

Here's why this matters:

- Failure gives us valuable information about what doesn't work.

- It helps us refine our approach and strategies.

- Each failure is a step closer to finding what does work.

Failure is not a stop sign. It's a detour sign guiding you to a better route.

Cultivate a growth mindset that views challenges as opportunities

Now, let's talk about mindset. There are two types: fixed and growth. A fixed mindset sees abilities as set in stone. A growth mindset, on the other hand, sees potential for development.

Guess which one helps us bounce back from failure? Yep, it's the growth mindset.

People with a growth mindset don't just tolerate challenges; they get excited by them. They see tough situations as chances to learn and improve. It's like they have special glasses that turn obstacles into opportunities.

So, how can we develop this superpower? Here are a few tricks:

1. Catch yourself when you're thinking in fixed terms. If you hear yourself say, "I'm just not good at this," try adding "yet" to the end.

2. Celebrate effort, not just results. Did you try something new and fail? Awesome! You just expanded your comfort zone.

3. Ask yourself, "What can I learn from this?" after every setback. It's like mining for gold in a pile of rubble.

Recognize that each failure brings you closer to success

Here's a mind-bending idea: What if success was a numbers game? What if you had to fail a certain number of times before you could succeed?

If that were true, wouldn't you want to get your failures out of the way as quickly as possible?

This isn't just a thought experiment. Many successful people attribute their achievements to the sheer number of attempts they made. They didn't succeed because they were smarter or more talented. They succeeded because they were willing to fail more often than others.

Think about it this way:

- Every failure eliminates one wrong way of doing things.

- Each attempt teaches you something new about your goal.

- The more you fail, the more experienced and knowledgeable you become.

Failure isn't just a step towards success. It's a necessary ingredient.

Thomas Edison's Lightbulb Moment

Let's talk about Thomas Edison for a second. You know, the guy who invented the lightbulb? 1,000 unsuccessful attempts before finally creating a working lightbulb. One thousand! Can you imagine trying something a thousand times and not giving up?

But here's a key takeaway. When someone asked him how it felt to fail 1,000 times, Edison said, "I will not say I failed 1,000 times; I will say that I found 1,000 ways that won't work."

Talk about a plot twist!

Edison saw each failed attempt as a step forward, not backward. He understood that each "failure" was actually bringing him closer to his goal.

Now, I'm not saying you need to fail a thousand times to succeed. But Edison's story teaches us some pretty cool lessons:

1. Persistence pays off. Edison didn't give up after the 10th try, or the 100th, or even the 999th. He kept going.

2. Failure is a form of progress. Each failed attempt taught Edison something new about what didn't work, narrowing down the possibilities of what might work.

3. Perspective is everything. By reframing his failures as discoveries, Edison maintained his motivation and enthusiasm.

So, the next time you're feeling down about a failure, channel your inner Edison. Ask yourself, "What have I discovered that doesn't work?" You might be surprised at how empowering that simple shift in perspective can be.

Wrapping It Up

Failure isn't a roadblock. It's a stepping stone. A teacher. A guide. It's your North Star, always pointing you in the direction of growth and improvement.

By embracing failure as feedback, cultivating a growth mindset, and recognizing the value in each attempt, you're not just setting yourself up for success. You're redefining what success means.

So go ahead. Fail. Fail often and fail spectacularly. Because with each failure, you're not moving away from success. You're moving towards it, one valuable lesson at a time.

Remember, the only real failure is giving up. As long as you keep trying, keep learning, and keep growing, you're already succeeding. And who knows? Your next attempt might just be the one that lights up the world.

Unlikely Triumphs

Let's look at some stories that'll blow your mind. We're talking about folks who hit rock bottom but didn't stay there. These people turned their big whoops into even bigger wins. Ready? Let's go!

J.K. Rowling: From Broke to Billionaire

Imagine being so poor you can't afford to heat your apartment. That was J.K. Rowling back in the day. She was a single mom on welfare, fighting depression, and trying to write a book about a boy wizard.

Here's the kicker: 12 publishers said "no thanks" to Harry Potter. Can you believe it? But Rowling didn't give up. She kept pushing, and finally, someone saw the magic in her words.

Now, Harry Potter is a global phenomenon. Books, movies, theme parks - you name it. Rowling went from struggling to pay rent to being richer than the King of England!

What can we learn from Rowling?

- Rejection isn't the end. It's just a "not yet."

- Your current situation doesn't define your future.

- Sometimes, the best ideas come when life is tough.

Steve Jobs: The Comeback Kid

Next up, let's talk about Steve Jobs. You know, the Apple guy. But did you know he got fired from his own company? Yep, the board of directors gave him the boot in 1985.

Most people would've thrown in the towel. But not Jobs. He started a new company called NeXT. He also bought Pixar (yeah, the folks who made Toy Story).

Then, plot twist! Apple bought NeXT in 1997, bringing Jobs back home. He went on to lead Apple to create some of the most game-changing products ever - the iPod, iPhone, and iPad.

Jobs once said, "Getting fired from Apple was the best thing that could have ever happened to me."

Here's what Jobs teaches us:

- Setbacks can lead to unexpected opportunities.

- Sometimes, you need to step back to leap forward.

- Your greatest success might come after your biggest failure.

Walt Disney: The Man Behind the Mouse

Now, let's rewind to the early 1900s. Meet Walt Disney, a young guy with big dreams and empty pockets. His first animation company? Bankrupt. His character, Oswald the Lucky Rabbit? Stolen by his distributor.

Ouch, right? But Walt didn't throw in the towel. Instead, he created a new character: Mickey Mouse. Maybe you've heard of him?

Disney faced rejection after rejection. People said his ideas were too wild and too expensive. But he kept pushing. Today, Disney is a global empire of movies, theme parks, and more.

What can we learn from Walt?

- Don't let early failures stop you.

- If someone steals your rabbit, make a mouse!

- Big dreams often face big obstacles. Keep dreaming anyway.

Now, let's zoom in on one incredible story. Buckle up because Oprah Winfrey's journey is one heck of a ride.

Oprah Winfrey: From Hardship to Media Queen

Picture this: A little girl born into poverty in rural Mississippi. Her childhood? Rough doesn't even begin to cover it. Oprah faced abuse, became pregnant at 14 (her son died in infancy), and was sent to live with her strict father in Nashville.

But here's where things get interesting. Oprah didn't let her past define her future. She started working in radio while still in high school. Then came her big break in TV news.

But wait, there's more! Oprah got fired from her first TV job as an anchor in Baltimore. The reason? They said she was "unfit for television news."

Unfit for television? Oh, the irony!

Instead of giving up, Oprah pivoted. She moved to a daytime TV show format, where she could be herself. And boy, did that work out!

The Oprah Winfrey Show became the highest-rated talk show in TV history. It ran for 25 years, people! That's longer than some of you have been alive.

But Oprah didn't stop there. She built a media empire:

- Her own production company

- A magazine

- A TV network (OWN - Oprah Winfrey Network)

- Book clubs that turn unknown authors into bestsellers overnight

And let's not forget her acting career. She was nominated for an Oscar for her very first movie role in *The Color Purple*.

Today, Oprah is one of the richest self-made women in America. She's also known for her philanthropy, giving millions to causes she believes in.

So, what can we learn from Oprah's incredible journey?

1. Your past doesn't determine your future. Oprah's childhood was tough, but she didn't let it hold her back.

2. Failure can point you in the right direction. Getting fired led Oprah to find her true calling.

3. Be yourself. Oprah's success came when she stopped trying to fit into someone else's mold.

4. Keep growing. Oprah didn't rest on her talk show success. She kept expanding her reach and trying new things.

5. Use your success to help others. Oprah's philanthropy shows that true success isn't just about personal gain.

The Big Picture

So, what do all these stories tell us? They show us that failure isn't the end. It's often just the beginning of something amazing.

These folks - Rowling, Jobs, Disney, and Oprah - they're not superheroes. They're regular people who faced big setbacks. But instead of giving up, they kept going. They learned from their failures, adapted, and came back stronger.

Here's the deal: Success isn't a straight line. It's more like a roller coaster with lots of ups and downs. The key is to enjoy the ride and learn from every twist and turn.

So, next time you face a setback, remember these stories. Remember that your "failure" might just be setting you up for something bigger and better than you ever imagined.

Who knows? Maybe one day, people will be reading about your unlikely triumph. So keep pushing, keep dreaming, and most importantly, keep going. Your best chapter might be just around the corner.

Your Growth Roadmap Awaits

Let's talk about something cool: your failure resume. No, that's not a typo. We're not talking about your regular resume that lists all your wins. We're talking about a special document that celebrates your whoopsies, your oops moments, and your face plants.

Sounds weird, right? But stick with me. This failure resume might just be your ticket to success.

What's a Failure Resume Anyway?

Think of it as a highlight reel of your lowlights. It's a record of times things didn't go as planned and what you learned from them. It's like keeping a diary, but instead of writing about your crush, you're writing about your crashes.

Here's how to make one:

1. Date: When did the flop happen?

2. Failure: What went wrong?

3. Lessons Learned: What did you figure out from this mess-up?

4. Next Steps: How will you use this info moving forward?

It's that simple. But don't let its simplicity fool you. This little tool can pack a big punch in your personal growth journey.

Keeping Your Failure Resume Fresh

Now, you might be thinking, "Great, I'll make this once and forget about it." Nope! Your failure resume is a living document. It should grow and change as you do.

Set a reminder on your phone. Every month or so, take a look at your failure resume. Add new stumbles. See if you've learned new lessons from old failures. It's like watering a plant - give it regular attention and watch it grow.

Why bother? Because reviewing your failures regularly does something magical to your brain. It turns those uh-oh moments into aha moments. You start to see patterns. You notice how far you've come. And most importantly, you realize that failure isn't fatal - it's just part of the journey.

Finding the Hidden Treasure in Your Failures

Here's where things get really interesting. Your failure resume isn't just a list of oopsies. It's a treasure map.

As you review your failures, you might notice some patterns. Maybe you often struggle with time management. Or perhaps you tend to avoid difficult conversations. These patterns are gold. They show you exactly where you need to focus to level up your game.

It's like having a personal coach pointing out your weak spots. Except this coach is free, available 24/7, and knows you better than anyone else - because it is you!

Now, let's see how this works in real life. Meet Zoe, a startup founder with big dreams and a few bumps along the way.

Zoe's Startup Saga: A Failure Resume in Action

Zoe always dreamed of starting her own tech company. Fresh out of college, full of energy and ideas, she dove right in. But things didn't go as smoothly as she hoped.

Her first entry in her failure resume looked like this:

Date: January 15, 2021

Failure: Launched app without proper market research. Only 50 downloads in the first month.

Lessons Learned: Enthusiasm isn't enough. Need to understand the target market better.

Next Steps: Learn how to conduct effective market research.

Ouch, right? But Zoe didn't let this stop her. She learned about market research, tweaked her app, and tried again.

A few months later, another entry:

Date: April 3, 2021

Failure: Ran out of funds. Had to let go of two team members.

Lessons Learned: Need better financial planning and forecasting.

Next Steps: Take an online course on startup finances.

This one hurt. Zoe loved her team. Instead of giving up, she used this setback to become smarter about money.

As months went by, Zoe's failure resume grew. But so did her skills and her resilience. Here's an entry from later that year:

Date: November 20, 2021

Failure: Missed chance to partner with a major company. Couldn't decide fast enough.

Lessons Learned: Need to trust my instincts more. Overthinking leads to missed opportunities.

Next Steps: Practice making quicker decisions on smaller issues to build confidence.

See how Zoe's failures were teaching her valuable lessons? She was learning about market research, finances, and decision-making, all crucial skills for a startup founder.

But here's where it gets really good. One day, Zoe sat down to review her failure resume. As she looked over her entries, she noticed something:

- Many of her failures involved acting too quickly without enough information.

- However, some involved being too slow to act when opportunities arose.

- She realized she needed to find a balance - gather enough info to make informed decisions but not get paralyzed by overthinking.

This was a huge aha moment for Zoe. She started working on finding the sweet spot between impulsiveness and indecision. And guess what? Her next app launch was a hit!

Two years after starting her failure resume, Zoe made this entry:

Date: February 1, 2023

Failure: None to report this month!

Lessons Learned: Looking back, I can see how each failure prepared me for success. I'm not afraid of setbacks anymore - they're just chances to learn and grow.

Next Steps: Keep innovating, keep learning, and keep updating this failure resume!

Zoe's story shows us the power of the failure resume. It's not just about recording failures - it's about transforming them into stepping stones for success.

Your Turn to Shine

So, are you ready to start your own failure resume? It's not about beating yourself up. It's about learning, growing, and becoming the awesome person you're meant to be.

Here's a quick recap:

1. Structure your failure resume with the date, failure, lessons learned, and next steps.

2. Update and review it regularly. Set a reminder if you need to.

3. Look for patterns. They're like secret messages from your experiences, showing you where to focus.

4. Use what you learn to make better decisions and take smarter risks.

Your failure resume isn't a record of your shortcomings. It's a roadmap for your growth. It's proof that you're brave enough to try, smart enough to learn, and strong enough to keep going.

So, go ahead and embrace your failures. Write them down. Learn from them. And watch as they transform from stumbling blocks into stepping stones on your path to success.

Remember, every big win has a backstory of failures. Your failure resume is just the rough draft of your success story. So start writing, and let's see where your journey takes you!

Rewrite Your Inner Dialogue for Success

Alright, let's dive into the wild world of what's going on in your head. You know that little voice that pipes up when things go wrong? The one that says, "Nice going, dummy!" Yeah, that one. We're going to teach it some new tricks.

Here's the deal: What you say to yourself matters. A lot. It's like having a personal cheerleader or a grumpy critic following you around all day. And guess what? You get to choose which one you want.

Identify and Challenge Self-Limiting Beliefs

First things first, we need to catch those sneaky self-limiting beliefs. They're like ninjas, slipping into your thoughts when you least expect it. "I'm not good enough." "I always mess up." "I'll never succeed." Sound familiar?

Here's how to catch these belief ninjas:

1. Pay attention to your thoughts, especially when things don't go as planned.

2. Write them down. Yep, grab a pen and paper. Make those sneaky thoughts visible.

3. Now, here's the fun part: Challenge them! Ask yourself, "Is this really true? Always? For everyone?"

For example, if you catch yourself thinking, "I always mess up," challenge it. Have you really messed up every single thing you've ever done? Probably not. Maybe you've messed up sometimes, but not always. See the difference?

Practice Positive Affirmations and Self-Compassion

Now that we've caught those pesky negative thoughts, let's replace them with something better. Enter positive affirmations and self-compassion.

Positive affirmations are like giving your brain a pep talk. Instead of "I always mess up," try "I learn and grow from my experiences." Instead of "I'm not good enough," how about "I am capable of improving and succeeding."

But here's the secret sauce: self-compassion. It's like being your own best friend. When you mess up, instead of beating yourself up, talk to yourself like you would to a friend who's having a tough time.

"Hey, it's okay. Everyone makes mistakes. What can you learn from this?"

Sounds cheesy? Maybe. But it works. Research shows that people who practice self-compassion are more resilient and happier. So go ahead and give yourself a mental hug.

Develop a Personal Mantra for Overcoming Setbacks

Now, let's create your secret weapon: a personal mantra. This is a short, powerful phrase you can use when things get tough. It's like a reset button for your brain.

Here are some examples:

- "I've got this."

- "Every setback is a setup for a comeback."

- "I am resilient and capable."

Pick one that resonates with you, or create your own. The key is to make it short, positive, and meaningful to you.

Now, let's see how this works in real life. Meet Jake, a professional basketball player who used to struggle with performance anxiety.

Jake's Journey: From Self-Doubt to Slam Dunks

Jake was always talented, but when the pressure was on, he'd freeze up. His inner critic would start yapping: "You're going to miss. Everyone's watching. Don't mess up!"

Result? He'd often miss shots he could usually make in his sleep.

One day, Jake decided enough was enough. He started working with a sports psychologist to rewrite his inner dialogue. Here's what he shared in an interview:

"I realized I was my own worst enemy on the court. Every time I messed up, I'd beat myself up. It was like I had this angry coach in my head, always yelling at me.

So, I started to change the conversation. Instead of 'Don't mess up,' I'd tell myself, 'You've practiced this shot a thousand times. Trust your training.'

I also came up with a mantra: 'Breathe, believe, achieve.' I'd repeat it to myself before every game and during tough moments.

The biggest change, though, was learning to be kind to myself. If I missed a shot, instead of calling myself names, I'd say, 'Okay, adjust and try again.' It felt weird at first, but man, did it make a difference.

Now, when I step onto the court, I feel confident. Sure, I still miss shots sometimes. But I don't let it shake me. I breathe, I believe, and more often than not, I achieve."

Jake's story shows us the power of rewriting our inner dialogue. He went from being paralyzed by self-doubt to performing at his peak, all by changing the conversation in his head.

Recap of Key Points

Let's break it down:

1. Failure isn't a dead end; it's a detour. Every successful person has a history of failures.

2. Your failure resume is your secret weapon. It turns setbacks into lessons.

3. What you say to yourself matters. A lot. Positive self-talk isn't just feel-good fluff; it's a performance enhancer.

4. Catching and challenging negative thoughts, practicing self-compassion, and having a personal mantra can transform your mindset and performance.

Action Steps

Ready to put this into action? Here's what you can do:

1. Start your failure resume today. Write down three recent setbacks and what you learned from them.

2. Think of a recent failure. Now, try to reframe it as an opportunity. What good could come from this?

3. Practice positive self-talk every day. Catch yourself when you're being negative and flip the script.

4. Pick someone you admire and research their failures. You might be surprised at what you find!

What's Next?

We've learned how to make friends with failure and give our inner critic a makeover. But knowing is only half the battle. In the next chapter, we're going to roll up our sleeves and get practical. We'll explore how to turn all this good mindset stuff into real, tangible habits that'll skyrocket you toward success.

Get ready to transform your thoughts into action. It's going to be one heck of a ride!

Chapter Five

The Gratitude Revolution: From Scarcity to Abundance Mindset

Rewiring Our Minds

Ever wonder why some people seem to radiate positivity while others struggle to find the silver lining? The answer might be simpler than you think. It's all about gratitude, and it's not just feel-good mumbo jumbo. Science is backing this up big time.

Let's explore the fascinating world of how gratitude can literally rewire our brains. Buckle up because this is going to blow your mind!

First things first: gratitude isn't just saying "thanks" when someone holds the door open for you. It's a whole mindset, a way of looking at the world that can change everything. And here's the pertinent point: it actually changes your brain.

When we practice gratitude, our brains release two important chemicals: dopamine and serotonin. These are like the body's natural feel-good drugs. Dopamine makes us feel rewarded and motivated, while serotonin helps regulate our mood and social behavior.

But it gets even better. The more we practice gratitude, the more our brains get used to releasing these chemicals. It's like we're creating a superhighway for positive thoughts. The brain is pretty lazy - it likes to take the path of least resistance. So, if we keep using this gratitude highway, it becomes our brain's go-to route.

Now, let's talk about two important parts of our brain:

1. The prefrontal cortex

2. The amygdala

The prefrontal cortex is like the brain's CEO. It's in charge of decision-making and emotional regulation. When we practice gratitude, this part of our brain becomes more active. It's like we're giving our inner CEO a power boost.

On the flip side, gratitude reduces activity in the amygdala. The amygdala is like our brain's security guard - always on the lookout for danger. It's linked to stress and fear responses. When we're grateful, this part of our brain calms down. It's like telling our inner security guard to take a chill pill.

But wait, there's more! Gratitude also enhances neuroplasticity. Don't let the big word scare you; it just means our brain's ability to change and adapt. When we practice gratitude, our brains become more flexible. This makes it easier for us to form positive thought patterns.

Now, I know what you're thinking. "This sounds great, but does it really work?"

Let me tell you a story about Dr. Mia Thompson, a neuroscientist who was pretty skeptical about all this gratitude stuff.

Dr. Thompson had been studying brain scans for years. She thought gratitude practices were just another fad. But then she decided to do a study on long-term gratitude practitioners. What she saw in their brain scans shocked her.

The gratitude practitioners showed:

- Increased activity in the prefrontal cortex

- Reduced activity in the amygdala

- More connections between different parts of the brain

Dr. Thompson was blown away. She decided to try gratitude practices herself. After just a few weeks, she noticed changes in her own mood and outlook. She became less stressed and more optimistic.

But the real results came when she scanned her own brain. The changes were there, clear as day. Dr. Thompson went from being a skeptic to one of the biggest advocates for gratitude practices in the scientific community.

So, what does all this mean for you? It means that gratitude isn't just some fluffy, feel-good exercise. It's a powerful tool that can actually change your brain. And the best part? It's free, and you can start right now.

Here's a simple gratitude exercise to get you started:

1. Every night before bed, think of three things you're grateful for.

2. They can be big things (like your health) or small things (like a good cup of coffee).

3. Really focus on each thing and why you're grateful for it.

4. Do this for at least two weeks and see how you feel.

Changing your brain takes time and practice. It's like going to the gym - you won't see results overnight, but if you stick with it, the changes will come.

Now, I can hear some of you saying, "But what if my life really sucks right now? How can I be grateful?"

That's a fair question. When life throws us curveballs, it can be hard to find things to be grateful for. But that's when gratitude is most powerful.

Try this: Start small. Maybe you're grateful for the air you breathe or the fact that you woke up this morning. Maybe you're grateful for the stranger who smiled at you on the street. These small moments of gratitude can be the first steps towards rewiring your brain.

The key is consistency. Even if you don't feel it at first, keep practicing gratitude. Your brain will catch up. Remember Dr. Thompson; even she was skeptical at first.

As you practice gratitude, you might start to notice some changes:

- You might feel happier and more content.

- You might handle stress better.

- You might find it easier to see the positive side of things.

- Your relationships might improve.

These changes aren't magic - they're the result of your brain rewiring itself. You're creating new neural pathways, strengthening your prefrontal cortex, and calming your amygdala.

In essence, you're shifting from a scarcity mindset to an abundance mindset. Instead of focusing on what you lack, you start to see all the good things in your life. And the more you practice, the easier it becomes.

So, are you ready to start your own gratitude revolution? Remember, it's not about changing your life overnight. It's about small, consistent steps that add up over time. Your brain is incredibly adaptable; give it the right input, and it will change.

Start today. What are you grateful for right now?

Gratitude's Hidden Corners in Everyday Life

We've all heard about being grateful for the big stuff: family, health, and a roof over our heads. But what if I told you that the real magic happens when you start finding gratitude in the nooks and crannies of your everyday life? Even in the tough spots. Especially in the tough spots.

Let's consider this idea. It's like turning on a light in a dark room - suddenly, you see things you never noticed before.

First off, let's talk about those tricky relationships. You know the ones - maybe it's that coworker who always seems to rub you the wrong way or that family member who knows just how to push your buttons. Here's a wild thought: what if you could find something to be grateful for in those relationships?

Now, I'm not saying you should be thankful for bad behavior. But maybe that difficult coworker has taught you patience. Maybe that challenging family member has helped you set better boundaries. When you start looking for these hidden lessons, you're not just practicing gratitude; you're growing as a person.

Here's a little exercise for you:

1. Think of a difficult relationship in your life.

2. Ask yourself: What have I learned from this relationship?

3. How has it made me stronger or more resilient?

4. Can I find one small thing to appreciate about this person?

It's not easy, but give it a try. You might be surprised at what you discover.

Now, let's talk about something we all deal with: physical discomfort. Whether it's a headache, sore muscles after a workout, or just the aches and pains of getting older, it's easy to focus on the negative. But what if we flipped the script?

That headache? It's a sign your body is telling you something; maybe you need more water or rest. Those sore muscles? They're proof that you're getting stronger. The creaky joints? They've carried you through life's adventures.

When we start seeing our body's signals as helpful information rather than just annoyances, we open up a whole new world of gratitude. It's like your body is constantly sending you little love notes; you just need to learn how to read them.

Try this: Next time you feel physical discomfort, take a moment to thank your body for communicating with you. It might feel weird at first, but stick with it. You're building a better relationship with yourself.

Now, let's tackle a big one: career setbacks. Losing a job, getting passed over for a promotion, or watching a project you poured your heart into fail - these things can feel devastating. But here's where gratitude can be a game-changer.

Every setback is a setup for a comeback. That's not just a catchy phrase; it's a mindset that can transform your career and your life. When you're able to find gratitude in these tough moments, you're giving yourself the gift of growth.

Let's break it down:

- Losing a job? Be grateful for the skills you gained and the network you built.

- Missed promotion? Thank the experience for showing you where you need to improve.

- Failed project? Appreciate all the lessons learned that will make your next project even better.

It's not about denying the pain or disappointment. It's about finding the silver lining that will propel you forward.

Now, I know what you're thinking. "This all sounds great in theory, but does it really work in the real world?"

Let me tell you a story about Amy, a corporate executive I worked with. Amy was facing a major company restructuring. Her team was being downsized, projects were being cut, and the stress was through the roof.

At first, Amy was overwhelmed. She couldn't see past the challenges. But then she decided to try something different. Every day, she started writing down three things she was grateful for about the situation.

At first, it was hard. However, as the days went by, Amy started to see things differently. She was grateful for the following:

1. The chance to learn new skills as she adapted to the changes.

2. The stronger bonds she was forming with her remaining team members.

3. The opportunity to reassess her career goals and what really mattered to her.

As Amy practiced this gratitude exercise, something remarkable happened. Her stress levels went down. She started coming up with innovative solutions to the restructuring challenges. Her team, inspired by her positive attitude, became more productive and cohesive.

By the end of the restructuring, Amy had not only survived; she had thrived. She was promoted to a higher position, largely due to her leadership during the challenging time.

The key takeaway? Amy credits her gratitude practice for giving her the perspective and resilience to turn a potential career disaster into a major win.

Now, I'm not saying gratitude will magically solve all your problems. But it can change how you see those problems, and that can change everything.

Here's the thing about gratitude in these hidden corners of life: it's not about ignoring the negative. It's about finding balance. It's about acknowledging the tough stuff while also recognizing the good.

When you start looking for things to be grateful for, even in challenging situations, you're training your brain to see opportunities instead of just obstacles. You're building resilience. You're becoming more adaptable.

And here's a secret: the more you practice gratitude in these hidden corners, the easier it becomes to find it everywhere. It's like you're developing a gratitude superpower.

So, how do you start? Here are some simple steps:

1. Set a daily reminder to find gratitude in an unexpected place.

2. Keep a gratitude journal, but challenge yourself to include at least one "tough" thing you're grateful for each day.

3. Share your hidden gratitude with others. It might inspire them to do the same.

This isn't about forcing positivity or denying real challenges. It's about expanding your perspective. It's about finding the lessons, the growth opportunities, and yes, even the blessings in disguise that are hiding in plain sight.

As you practice this, you might notice some changes. You might become more resilient in the face of challenges. You might find it easier to connect with difficult people. You might even start to see "failures" as valuable feedback rather than devastating setbacks.

In essence, you're not just practicing gratitude; you're transforming your entire approach to life. You're moving from a scarcity mindset ("Everything's going wrong") to an abundance mindset ("There's something to learn and appreciate in every situation").

So, are you ready to start exploring the hidden corners of gratitude in your life? Remember, it's a practice. It might feel awkward or forced at first. But stick with it. The more you look for things to be grateful for, the more you'll find. And that can change everything.

Reshaping Your Mental Landscape

Ever feel like your brain is stuck on a loop of negative thoughts? Like no matter how hard you try, you just can't shake off that gloomy cloud hanging over your head?

Welcome to the world of intentional gratitude practices. It's like going to the gym, but it's for your mind. And just like working out can transform your body, these practices can reshape your mental landscape.

Let's start with the basics. Gratitude isn't just about saying "thanks" when someone holds the door open for you. It's a way of looking at the world, of actively seeking out the good in your life. And when you do this consistently, day after day, something amazing happens. Your brain starts to change.

Now, I know what you're thinking. "Change my brain? That sounds complicated." But here's the thing: your brain is changing all the time. Every thought you have and every experience you go through shapes your neural pathways. So why not take control of that process?

Let's think about some practical ways to do just that.

First up: Morning gratitude journaling. This is like a cup of coffee for your soul. Before you check your phone, before you start worrying about your to-do list, take a few minutes to write down three things you're grateful for.

Here's how to do it:

1. Keep a notebook and pen by your bed.

2. As soon as you wake up, write down three specific things you're grateful for.

3. They can be big or small - from "I'm grateful for my family" to "I'm grateful for the cozy blanket I slept under last night."

4. Be specific. Instead of "I'm grateful for my job," try "I'm grateful for the way my coworker helped me with that tricky project yesterday."

This practice sets the tone for your entire day. It's like putting on a pair of gratitude glasses that help you see the good in everything.

Next up: Gratitude walks. This is a great way to combine physical exercise with mental training. Plus, it gets you out in nature, which is its own mood booster.

Here's how it works:

1. Go for a walk - it can be in your neighborhood, a park, or anywhere you like.

2. As you walk, focus on appreciating your surroundings.

3. Notice the warmth of the sun on your skin, the sound of birds chirping, and the feel of the ground beneath your feet.

4. Try to find at least five things to be grateful for during your walk.

This practice helps you become more present and aware of the good things that surround you every day. It's like a gratitude scavenger hunt!

Finally, let's talk about evening reflection. This is a great way to bookend your day with gratitude.

Here's what to do:

1. Before you go to bed, think back on your day.

2. Identify three specific moments you're grateful for.

3. They don't have to be big moments - maybe you're grateful for the delicious lunch you had, the funny meme a friend sent you, or the satisfaction of crossing something off your to-do list.

4. Really savor these moments. Relive them in your mind.

This practice helps you end your day on a positive note, no matter what challenges you face. It's like giving your brain a little pep talk before bed.

Now, I know what some of you might be thinking. "This all sounds great, but I'm just not a naturally positive person. I'm more of a glass-half-empty kind of guy."

Let's look at Mike's case. If it were sunny, he'd complain about the glare. If it were raining, he'd grumble about the mud. His friends used to joke that he could find the cloud in every silver lining.

But then Mike decided to try something different. He committed to 30 days of gratitude practice. At first, it was a struggle. He felt silly writing down things he was grateful for. His gratitude walks felt forced and unnatural. But he stuck with it.

By the end of the first week, Mike noticed something strange. He caught himself smiling at a butterfly that landed on his window. He actually enjoyed the sound of rain on his roof.

By the end of the second week, his coworkers started to comment on his improved mood. He was more pleasant to be around and more willing to help out on projects.

By the end of the 30 days, Mike was a changed man. He still had bad days, of course - gratitude isn't magic. But he had the tools to deal with those bad days. He could find the silver lining in tough situations. His whole outlook on life had shifted.

The best part? Mike's transformation didn't just affect him. His improved attitude rubbed off on his family and his friends; even his dog seemed happier! It was like he had started a positive ripple effect.

Now, you might be wondering, "Does this really work for everyone?" The answer is yes, but with a caveat. Like any skill, gratitude takes practice. You might feel awkward or insincere at first. That's okay. Keep at it.

Think of it like learning a new language. At first, you might stumble over the words and feel self-conscious about your accent. But the more you practice, the more natural it becomes. Eventually, you start thinking in that new language.

It's the same with gratitude. At first, you might have to really search for things to be grateful for. But over time, it becomes second nature. You start to notice the good things in your life automatically.

Here's the science behind why this works: When you practice gratitude regularly, you're actually creating new neural pathways in your brain. You're training your mind to look for the positive. It's like you're creating a superhighway for positive thoughts, making it easier and faster for your brain to access them.

But here's the key: consistency. Reshaping your mental landscape isn't a one-and-done deal. It's something you need to work on every day. But the good news is the more you do it, the easier it gets.

So, are you ready to start reshaping your mental landscape? Here's a challenge for you: Try one of these gratitude practices every day for the next week. It doesn't matter which one you choose - morning journaling, gratitude walks, or evening reflection. Just pick one and stick with it for seven days.

At the end of the week, take stock. How do you feel? Has your outlook changed at all? Are you noticing more positive things in your life?

This isn't about ignoring the negative things in your life or pretending everything is perfect. It's about balancing your perspective. It's about training your brain to see the good alongside the bad.

And here's a little secret: The more you practice gratitude, the more things you'll find to be grateful for. It's like you're tuning your brain to a different frequency: the gratitude frequency. And once you're tuned in, you'll be amazed at what you hear.

So go ahead and give it a try. Your future, more grateful self will thank you for it.

The Abundance Awakening

You know that feeling when you're running low on cash, and suddenly, every expense feels like a punch to the gut? That's scarcity thinking in action. It's like wearing blinders that only let you see what you lack. But what if I told you there's a way to take those blinders off and see the world of abundance all around you?

Welcome to the abundance awakening. It's not about magically making more money appear in your bank account (though that can be a nice side effect). It's about shifting your entire perspective on what you have and what's possible.

Let's start by talking about those pesky limiting beliefs. These are the sneaky little thoughts that whisper things like "There's never enough" or "Good things don't happen to people like me." They're like weeds in the garden of your mind, choking out the possibility of abundance.

Here's a quick exercise to identify your limiting beliefs:

1. Take a piece of paper and draw a line down the middle.

2. On one side, write "What I want." This could be more money, better relationships, or career success.

3. On the other side, write "Why I can't have it." Be honest about your fears and doubts.

4. Look at the "Why I can't have it" side. These are your limiting beliefs.

Now that you've identified these beliefs, it's time to challenge them. For each limiting belief, ask yourself:

- Is this really true?

- What evidence do I have that contradicts this belief?

- How would my life be different if I didn't believe this?

This process of questioning your limiting beliefs is like pulling up those weeds by the roots. It clears space for abundance to grow.

Next, let's talk about abundance affirmations and visualizations. These are like planting seeds of abundance in your mind.

Here are some powerful abundance affirmations:

- "I am open to receiving abundance in all areas of my life."

- "There is more than enough for everyone, including me."

- "I attract opportunities and resources easily and effortlessly."

Repeat these affirmations daily, preferably in front of a mirror. It might feel silly at first, but stick with it. You're rewiring your brain to expect abundance.

For visualizations, try this:

1. Close your eyes and imagine your life filled with abundance.

2. What does it look like? Feel like? Sound like?

3. Really immerse yourself in this vision.

4. Do this for 5-10 minutes each day.

Your brain doesn't know the difference between what's real and what's vividly imagined. By regularly visualizing abundance, you're training your mind to look for and create that abundance in your real life.

Now, here's where things get really interesting. One of the most powerful ways to reinforce an abundance mindset is by sharing resources and opportunities with others. It sounds counterintuitive, right? If you're trying to attract more abundance, shouldn't you hold onto what you have?

Actually, the opposite is true. When you share from a place of abundance, you're sending a powerful message to your subconscious (and the universe) that there's more than enough to go around. It's like turning on a tap of abundance that flows both ways.

Try this:

- Share a useful piece of information with a colleague.

- Introduce two friends who could benefit from knowing each other.

- Donate to a cause you care about, even if it's just a small amount.

Each time you do this, remind yourself: "There's always more where that came from."

Now, I know what you're thinking. "This all sounds great, but does it really work in the real world?"

Let me tell you about Eliza, a small business owner I worked with. Eliza ran a local bakery, and for years, she was constantly stressed about money. She pinched every penny, worried about every slow day, and was always bracing for financial disaster.

Then Eliza decided to try cultivating an abundance mindset. She started with daily gratitude practices, focusing on appreciating what she already had. She challenged her limiting beliefs about money and success. She started visualizing her bakery thriving and growing.

However, the real turning point came when Eliza decided to start giving away free samples of her baked goods to local charities. It felt scary at first - giving away products when money was tight? But Eliza committed to it, reminding herself that there was always more than enough.

Something amazing started to happen. People who tried her samples at charity events started coming to the bakery. Word spread about her generosity, and community support grew. A local newspaper did a feature on her, bringing in even more customers.

Within six months, Eliza's bakery was doing better than ever. She was able to hire more staff, expand her menu, and even start planning for a second location. But more than that, Eliza's whole outlook on life had changed. She no longer lived in fear of scarcity. She operated from a place of abundance, and it showed in everything she did.

The best part? Eliza's abundance mindset started rubbing off on her employees and customers. Her bakery became known not just for great pastries but for its positive, generous atmosphere. It was like she had started a ripple effect of abundance in her community.

Now, I'm not saying that cultivating an abundance mindset will automatically make all your problems disappear. But it can change how you approach those problems. It can open your eyes to opportunities you might have missed before. It can make you more resilient, more creative, and more open to possibilities.

Here's a quick recap of the key points we've covered:

- Gratitude is the foundation of an abundance mindset. It helps you appreciate what you already have.

- Identifying and challenging limiting beliefs clears space for abundance thinking.

- Abundance affirmations and visualizations trains your brain to expect and create abundance.

- Sharing resources and opportunities reinforces the idea that there's more than enough to go around.

So, are you ready to start your own abundance awakening? Here are some action steps to get you started:

1. Start a daily gratitude journal. Each morning, list 3 to 5 things you're grateful for.

2. Choose one challenging area of your life and find three aspects to appreciate about it.

3. Implement a daily gratitude ritual, like a gratitude walk or evening reflection.

4. Identify one scarcity-based belief you have, challenge it, and replace it with an abundance affirmation.

Remember, shifting from scarcity to abundance thinking is a journey, not a destination. Be patient with yourself. Celebrate small wins. And most importantly, keep practicing.

As we wrap up this chapter on the gratitude revolution and abundance mindset, we've laid a strong foundation for overcoming self-doubt and limiting beliefs. In the next chapter, we'll build on this foundation as we explore mindfulness for the skeptic and practical ways to apply it in a busy world. Get ready to discover how to harness your newfound abundance mindset to fuel your journey toward living your most authentic, empowered life.

The path to abundance starts with a single step. Are you ready to take that step?

Chapter Six

Mindfulness for the Skeptic: Practical Applications in a Busy World

Unmasking Mindfulness Misconceptions

Let's face it - mindfulness has a bit of an image problem. For many people, the word conjures up images of cross-legged yogis chanting "Om" for hours on end. But here's the surprising truth: mindfulness is a practical, science-backed tool that can fit into even the busiest of lives.

It's time to bust some myths and get real about what mindfulness actually is and how it can work for you.

Myth #1: Mindfulness requires hours of meditation

This is probably the biggest misconception out there. Many people think they need to set aside huge chunks of time to practice mindfulness. The reality? You can practice mindfulness in as little as one minute.

Think about it like this: mindfulness is simply paying attention to the present moment. You can do that while:

- Brushing your teeth

- Waiting in line at the grocery store

- Walking from your car to your office

The key is to focus on your senses and what's happening right now rather than getting lost in thoughts about the past or future.

Meet Kate

Kate, a high-powered executive, used to roll her eyes at the mention of mindfulness. "I don't have time for that hippie stuff," she'd say. But when her stress levels started affecting her work, she decided to give it a shot.

Kate started small. She set a reminder on her phone to take three deep breaths before each meeting. That's it. Just three breaths, focusing on the sensation of air moving in and out of her lungs.

To her surprise, this tiny practice made a big difference. She felt more centered and focused in her meetings. Over time, she added more brief mindfulness moments to her day.

The result? Kate's productivity went up, and her stress levels went down, all without her having spent hours in meditation.

Myth #2: Mindfulness is only for "spiritual" people

Here's another whopper of a myth. You don't need to be spiritual or religious to benefit from mindfulness. In fact, mindfulness has been embraced by some pretty hard-nosed, results-driven organizations.

- The U.S. Marine Corps uses mindfulness training to improve soldiers' mental performance.

- Google offers mindfulness courses to its employees to boost creativity and productivity.

- The Seattle Seahawks football team practices mindfulness to enhance focus and teamwork.

These aren't exactly places you'd expect to find "spiritual" practices, right? That's because mindfulness is fundamentally about training your attention. It's a mental skill, not a belief system.

Myth #3: Mindfulness means emptying your mind completely

If you've ever tried to "empty your mind," you know how impossible that can feel. Good news: that's not what mindfulness is about.

Mindfulness isn't about having no thoughts. It's about noticing your thoughts without getting caught up in them.

Think of it like this: your mind is like a busy street. Thoughts are the cars driving by. Mindfulness is about sitting on a bench, watching the cars go by, without jumping into every vehicle that passes.

You're not trying to stop the traffic. You're just observing it.

Practical Mindfulness: A Skeptic's Guide

Now that we've busted some myths, let's talk about how to practice mindfulness in everyday life. This isn't about becoming a Zen master. It's about finding small ways to be more present and aware.

1. The One-Minute Breath Break

Set a timer for one minute. Close your eyes and focus on your breath. Notice the sensation of breathing in and out. When your mind wanders (and it will), gently bring your attention back to your breath.

Do this once a day, maybe right after lunch or before an important meeting. It's a quick reset for your mind.

2. The Sensory Commute

On your way to work, pick one sense to focus on. Maybe it's what you see; really notice the colors, shapes, and movements around you. Or focus on sounds; can you pick out individual noises in the general hum of your environment?

This turns a mundane daily activity into a mindfulness practice.

3. The Mindful Bite

At your next meal, take one bite with full attention. Notice the texture, flavor, and sensation of the food in your mouth. Chew slowly and really experience it.

This not only introduces a moment of mindfulness but can also help with digestion and enjoyment of your food.

4. The Body Scan

Before bed, lie down and mentally scan your body from head to toe. Notice any areas of tension or discomfort without trying to change them. This can help you relax and prepare for sleep.

5. The "Name That Emotion" Game

When you're feeling stressed or upset, take a moment to name the emotion you're experiencing. "I'm feeling frustrated right now." or "This is anxiety." Naming emotions can help create a bit of distance and perspective.

The Science Behind the Practice

If you're still skeptical, consider this: a growing body of scientific research supports the benefits of mindfulness. Studies have shown that regular mindfulness practice can:

- Reduce stress and anxiety

- Improve focus and memory

- Boost immune function

- Enhance emotional regulation

These aren't fluffy, feel-good claims. Brain scans, blood tests, and rigorous scientific methods back them.

For example, a study published in the journal *Psychiatry Research: Neuroimaging* found that after just eight weeks of mindfulness practice, participants showed increased gray matter density in brain regions associated with learning, memory, and emotional regulation.

Another study in the journal *Psychoneuroendocrinology* found that mindfulness meditation decreased inflammation markers in the blood, suggesting it could have positive effects on physical health.

The Bottom Line

Mindfulness isn't about becoming a different person or even a "better" person. It's about training your brain to be more aware and present in your everyday life. It's a practical tool that can help you navigate the challenges of modern life with more ease and less stress.

You don't need to overhaul your life or spend hours in meditation. Start small. Be consistent. And most importantly, be patient with yourself. Like any skill, mindfulness takes practice. But the benefits? They're worth every mindful moment.

Remember Kate? She started with just three breaths before meetings. Now, she swears by her daily mindfulness practice. "It's like a superpower," she says. "I feel more in control, more focused, and honestly, just happier."

So, skeptics, are you ready to give mindfulness a try? Your calmer, more focused self is waiting.

Mindfulness for Busy Lives

Let's be real. You're busy. We all are. The idea of squeezing in yet another thing to your jam-packed day might make you want to scream. But what if I told you that you could practice mindfulness without adding a single extra minute to your schedule? Sounds too good to be true, right? Because we're about to dive into the world of micro-mindfulness practices that can fit seamlessly into your hectic life.

The Power of Micro-Mindfulness

Think of mindfulness like taking a vitamin. You don't need to chug a whole bottle to get the benefits. A small, consistent dose can work wonders. That's where micro-mindfulness comes in. These are tiny practices that you can sprinkle throughout your day, like adding a dash of salt to your meal. A little goes a long way.

Meet John, the Frazzled Developer

Before we jump into the practices, let me tell you about John. John's a software developer who felt like his brain was a browser with 100 tabs open all the time. He was constantly switching between tasks, feeling frazzled and on the verge of burnout. Sound familiar?

John had heard about mindfulness but thought it was just another time-suck he couldn't afford. Then, he learned about micro-mindfulness practices. Here's how he used them to transform his workday:

1. The 60-Second Breath Awareness Exercise

This is the Swiss Army knife of mindfulness practices. It's quick and easy, and you can do it anywhere. Here's how:

- Set a timer for 60 seconds.

- Close your eyes (if it's safe to do so).

- Focus on your breath. Feel the air moving in and out.

- When your mind wanders (and it will), gently bring it back to your breath.

- When the timer goes off, take one last deep breath and return to your day.

John started doing this every time he switched tasks. It helped him clear his mental cache and refocus. He found he made fewer mistakes and felt less scattered.

2. Mindful Eating During Lunch Breaks

Let's face it: most of us eat lunch while staring at a screen. We barely taste our food, let alone enjoy it. Mindful eating can change that. Here's how John did it:

- He turned off his phone and closed his laptop.

- He looked at his food, noticing the colors and textures.

- He took a small bite and chewed slowly, really tasting the flavors.

- He paid attention to how the food felt in his mouth and as he swallowed.

- He did this for just the first few bites of his meal.

John found that this practice not only made his lunch more enjoyable but also gave his brain a much-needed break. He returned to work feeling refreshed and more focused.

3. Three-Minute Body Scan Before Bed

Sleep is crucial for mental clarity and emotional balance. But many of us struggle to switch off at night. That's where the body scan comes in. Here's John's routine:

- He lay in bed and closed his eyes.

- Starting from his toes, he mentally scanned up his body.

- He noticed any areas of tension or discomfort without trying to change them.

- He imagined breathing into each part of his body as he scanned.

- When he reached the top of his head, he took three deep breaths.

This practice helped John let go of the day's stress and prepare for sleep. He found he fell asleep faster and woke up feeling more rested.

The Ripple Effect of Micro-Mindfulness

Now, you might be thinking, "Sure, these sound nice, but do they really make a difference?" Let's look at what happened to John.

At first, the changes were subtle. He noticed he was a bit calmer during the day. He wasn't snapping at his coworkers as much. His code had fewer bugs.

But over time, these small changes added up to something big. John's productivity improved. His boss noticed and gave him more challenging projects. He started enjoying his work more.

The best part? John's stress levels dropped. He wasn't taking his work frustrations home with him. His relationships improved. He even started sleeping better.

All from a few minutes of mindfulness sprinkled throughout his day.

Making Micro-Mindfulness Work for You

Now, I know what you're thinking. "That's great for John, but my life is different." You're right. Your life is unique. So, let's talk about how to make micro-mindfulness work for you.

1. Start Small

Don't try to do all these practices at once. Pick one that appeals to you and start there. Maybe it's the breath awareness exercise. Try doing it once a day for a week. See how it feels.

2. Anchor Your Practice

Link your mindfulness practice to something you already do every day. For example:

- Do the breath awareness exercise every time you sit down at your desk.

- Practice mindful eating with your first bite at every meal.

- Do the body scan right after you brush your teeth at night.

This makes it easier to remember and turns it into a habit.

3. Be Consistent, Not Perfect

You'll forget sometimes. You'll get distracted. That's okay. The goal isn't perfection. It's consistency. If you miss a day, just start again the next day.

4. Experiment and Adjust

These practices are a starting point. Feel free to adjust them to fit your life. Maybe you prefer a two-minute breath exercise. Or perhaps you want to do a body scan in the morning instead of at night. Make it work for you.

5. Notice the Little Changes

Big transformations start with small shifts. Pay attention to the little things. Maybe you feel a bit calmer after your breath exercise. Or you enjoy your food more when you eat mindfully. Celebrate these small wins.

The Science Behind Micro-Mindfulness

If you're still skeptical, let's talk science for a moment. Studies have shown that even brief mindfulness practices can have significant benefits:

- A study in the journal *Mindfulness* found that just 10 minutes of mindfulness practice a day improved focus and reduced mind-wandering.

- Research published in *Psychological Science* showed that a brief mindfulness exercise before a task improved memory and cognitive performance.

- A study in the *Journal of Occupational Health Psychology* found that short, work-based mindfulness interventions reduced stress and improved job satisfaction.

These aren't fluffy, feel-good claims. They're backed by solid research.

Your Turn to Try

So, are you ready to give micro-mindfulness a shot? You don't need to overhaul your life. You don't need to sit in the lotus position for hours. You just need to bring a little more awareness to the moments you're already living.

Start small. Be consistent. And most importantly, be kind to yourself as you explore these practices.

Who knows? Like John, you might find that these tiny moments of mindfulness add up to big changes in your life. Less stress, more focus, better relationships, improved work performance, all from a few minutes of mindfulness sprinkled throughout your day.

So, take a deep breath. Feel the air moving in and out. Congratulations - you've just taken your first step into the world of micro-mindfulness. Welcome aboard!

Igniting Creative Solutions

Ever feel like your brain is stuck in a rut? Like you're facing a problem, and all you can see are brick walls? I know what you're thinking. "Mindfulness for creativity? Isn't that just for stress relief?" Nope. It's a secret weapon for innovative thinking, too. Let's dive into how you can use mindfulness to supercharge your creativity.

Mindful Brainstorming: Think Outside the Box (While Sitting In It)

Picture this: You're in a brainstorming session. Ideas are flying. But half the team is checking their phones, and the other half is thinking about lunch. Sound familiar?

Now, imagine starting that same meeting with a quick mindfulness exercise. Here's how:

1. Everyone closes their eyes (or looks at a neutral spot).

2. Take three deep breaths together.

3. Spend one minute noticing thoughts without judgment.

4. Take one more deep breath and open your eyes.

Seems simple, right? But here's where the magic happens. This little exercise helps everyone get present. It clears out the mental clutter and opens up space for new ideas to bloom.

Let's look at a real-life example. A small marketing team at a struggling startup was facing a major challenge. Their product wasn't selling, and they needed a fresh campaign fast. They decided to try starting their brainstorming sessions with a 10-minute mindfulness exercise.

The results? Mind-blowing. Team members reported feeling more focused and open. Ideas started flowing more freely. And the best part? The quality of ideas improved. They came up with a campaign that not only boosted sales but revitalized their entire brand.

Why does this work? Mindfulness helps quiet the inner critic that often shuts down our wildest (and sometimes best) ideas before we even share them. It creates a judgment-free zone where all ideas are welcome.

Meditation: Your Idea Incubator

Now, let's talk about using meditation to incubate ideas. This gives your brain some quiet time to connect the dots you might miss in the hustle and bustle of daily life.

Here's a simple technique:

1. Sit comfortably and close your eyes.

2. Focus on your breath for a few minutes.

3. Then, gently bring your challenge or problem to mind.

4. Don't try to solve it. Just hold it in your awareness.

5. If solutions pop up, notice them without grabbing on.

6. After 10-15 minutes, open your eyes and jot down any insights.

This practice is like planting seeds in your subconscious. You might not see results right away. But give it time, and those seeds will sprout into surprising solutions.

One CEO I know swears by this method. She was struggling with a complex business decision. After a week of daily "idea incubation" meditations, she woke up one morning with a clear solution. It was an approach she'd never considered before, but it turned out to be exactly what her company needed.

The Non-Judgmental Observer: Your Inner Idea Factory

Here's a mindfulness technique that can turn your inner critic into your biggest creative ally. It's called non-judgmental observation of thoughts.

How it works:

1. Sit quietly for a few minutes.

2. Notice the thoughts that pop into your head.

3. Don't judge them as good or bad; just observe.

4. If you catch yourself judging, that's okay. Just notice that, too.

This practice helps you see your thoughts as just thoughts, not facts. It creates some space between you and your ideas. And in that space, creativity can flourish.

Try this: Next time you're stuck on a problem, spend 5 minutes observing your thoughts about it without judgment. You might be surprised at the fresh perspectives that emerge.

One artist I know used this technique to overcome a creative block. She'd been staring at a blank canvas for weeks, paralyzed by self-doubt. After practicing non-judgmental observation, she realized many of her "I can't" thoughts were just old habits, not truths. This freed her to start experimenting again, leading to a breakthrough series of paintings.

The Science Behind Mindful Creativity

Now, I'm not just making this stuff up. There's solid science backing the link between mindfulness and creativity.

A study published in the journal *Mindfulness* found that even brief mindfulness exercises can boost divergent thinking; that's the kind of thinking that generates multiple, creative solutions to a problem.

Another study in the *Journal of Business Venturing* showed that entrepreneurs who practice mindfulness come up with more innovative ideas for new products.

Why does it work? Researchers think mindfulness helps in a few ways:

- It reduces stress, which can block creative thinking.

- It improves focus, helping you stay on task.

- It enhances cognitive flexibility, helping you see new connections.

Putting It All Together: Your Mindful Creativity Toolkit

So, how can you start using mindfulness to boost your creativity? Here's a simple toolkit to get you started:

1. Start your day with a 5-minute breath awareness exercise. This sets the tone for a more mindful, creative day.

2. Before tackling a tough problem, try a 10-minute "idea incubation" meditation.

3. When you're feeling stuck, take a mindful walk. Pay attention to your surroundings using all your senses. This can help shake loose new ideas.

4. End your day with 5 minutes of non-judgmental thought observation. This can help process the day's events and spark new insights.

Consistency is key. You might not see results overnight. But stick with it, and you'll likely notice your creative juices flowing more freely over time.

A Word of Caution

Now, I'm not saying mindfulness is a magic creativity pill. It's a tool, not a miracle worker. You still need to put in the work. You still need to face the blank page or the challenging problem. But mindfulness can help make that process smoother and more enjoyable.

Also, don't get discouraged if your mind wanders during these practices. That's normal. The practice is to notice the wandering and gently bring your attention back. Each time you do this, you're strengthening your "mental muscle" for focus and creativity.

Your Creative Adventure Awaits

So, are you ready to supercharge your creativity with mindfulness? Remember, you don't need to overhaul your entire life. Start small. Maybe try the mindful brainstorming technique in your next team meeting. Or spend 5 minutes doing a thought observation exercise before tackling your next big project.

Who knows? Like that marketing team we talked about, you might find that a little mindfulness goes a long way in sparking big ideas. Your next creative breakthrough could be just a few mindful breaths away.

Now, take a deep breath. Feel the air moving in and out. And let your mind wander to the possibilities that await when you combine the focus of mindfulness with the spark of your creativity. Exciting, isn't it? Your mindful, creative adventure starts now!

Rewire Your Inner Voice with Mindfulness

Ever feel like there's a little voice in your head that's always putting you down? You're not alone. We all have that inner critic. But here's the good news: you can change that voice. And mindfulness is the key.

Let's see how you can use mindfulness to turn your inner critic into your biggest cheer-leader.

Identifying Thought Patterns: The First Step to Freedom

You can't change what you don't notice. That's where mindfulness comes in. It's like turning on a light in a dark room. Suddenly, you can see what's been there all along.

Here's a simple exercise to get started:

1. Sit quietly for a few minutes.

2. Notice the thoughts that pop into your head.

3. Don't try to change them. Just observe.

4. If you catch yourself judging, that's okay. Just notice that, too.

The goal isn't to have no thoughts. It's to become aware of the thoughts you're having. You might be surprised at what you discover.

Meet Alex: The Reluctant Entrepreneur

Let's look at a real-life example. Alex had a great business idea, but he kept putting off launching his startup. Every time he thought about taking action, his mind flooded with doubts:

"What if it fails?"

"Who am I to think I can run a business?"

"I'm not ready yet."

Sound familiar? These thoughts kept Alex stuck for months. Then, he learned about mindful awareness.

Alex started spending 5 minutes each morning just noticing his thoughts. At first, it was uncomfortable. He realized just how often he put himself down. But over time, something amazing happened. He started to see these thoughts for what they were: just thoughts, not facts.

This awareness was the first step in Alex's journey to launching his business. But he didn't stop there.

The STOP Technique: Your Emergency Brake for Negative Thoughts

Sometimes, negative thoughts can feel like a runaway train. That's where the STOP technique comes in. It's like hitting the emergency brake on that train of thought. Here's how it works:

S - Stop what you're doing.

T - Take a breath.

O - Observe your thoughts and feelings.

P - Proceed with something that will support you.

Alex used this technique whenever he felt overwhelmed by self-doubt. Here's how it looked for him:

S - He'd stop working on his business plan.

T - He'd take a deep breath, feeling the air move in and out.

O - He'd notice his thoughts: "I'm not cut out for this." And his feelings: anxiety and fear.

P - He'd remind himself of why he wanted to start this business in the first place.

This simple practice helped Alex break the cycle of negative thinking. It gave him a moment of clarity to choose his next action rather than just reacting to his fears.

Cultivating Self-Compassion: Your Secret Weapon

Now, let's talk about self-compassion. It's not just about being nice to yourself. It's about treating yourself with the same kindness you'd offer a good friend.

One powerful way to build self-compassion is through loving-kindness meditation. Here's a simple version:

1. Sit comfortably and close your eyes.

2. Repeat these phrases to yourself:

"May I be happy."

"May I be healthy."

"May I be safe."

"May I live with ease."

3. As you say each phrase, really feel the intention behind it.

At first, this might feel awkward or even silly. That's okay. Stick with it. Over time, it can profoundly shift how you talk to yourself.

For Alex, this practice was a game-changer. He realized he'd never talk to a friend the way he talked to himself. This awareness helped him start treating himself with more kindness and understanding.

The Science Behind Mindful Self-Talk

Now, you might be thinking, "This all sounds nice, but does it really work?" Let's look at the science.

A study published in the journal *Clinical Psychology Review* found that self-compassion was strongly linked to lower levels of anxiety and depression.

Another study in the *Journal of Personality and Social Psychology* showed that people who practiced mindfulness were better able to let go of negative thoughts.

These aren't just feel-good findings. They're backed by solid research. Mindfulness can literally rewire your brain to be more resilient and positive.

Putting It All Together: Alex's Breakthrough

So, how did all this play out for Alex? Let's take a look:

- He started each day with 5 minutes of mindful awareness, noticing his thoughts without judgment.

- He used the STOP technique whenever he felt overwhelmed by self-doubt.

- He practiced loving-kindness meditation for 10 minutes each night before bed.

The results? They didn't happen overnight. But over time, Alex noticed big changes:

- He became more aware of his negative self-talk.

- He could pause and challenge his self-doubting thoughts.

- He started treating himself with more kindness and understanding.

These changes gave Alex the courage to take action. He finally launched his business. Was it perfect? No. Did everything go smoothly? Of course not. However, Alex was able to navigate the challenges with more resilience and self-confidence.

Your Turn: Rewiring Your Inner Voice

Ready to start rewiring your own inner voice? Here are some steps to get you started:

1. Practice mindful awareness: Spend 5 minutes each day just noticing your thoughts. Don't try to change them, just observe.

2. Use the STOP technique: Next time you're caught in a spiral of negative thoughts, try the STOP technique.

3. Cultivate self-compassion: Try the loving-kindness meditation for 5 minutes each day.

4. Be patient with yourself: you're undoing years of habit. It takes time. Be kind to yourself in the process.

A Word of Caution

Now, I'm not saying mindfulness will magically erase all your self-doubt. That's not the goal. Some self-doubt is normal and can even be helpful. The goal is to have a healthier relationship with that inner voice.

Also, if you're dealing with severe negative self-talk or depression, it's important to seek help from a mental health professional. Mindfulness can be a great tool, but it's not a substitute for professional help when you need it.

Your New Inner Cheerleader Awaits

So, are you ready to start transforming your inner critic into your biggest fan? Remember, this is a journey. There will be ups and downs. But with consistent practice, you can change that inner voice.

Imagine waking up each day with an inner voice that encourages you, supports you, and believes in you. That's the power of mindful self-talk.

Take a deep breath. Feel the air moving in and out. And as you exhale, let go of one negative thought about yourself. Replace it with a kind one. That's your first step on this exciting journey of self-discovery and growth.

Your new, more compassionate inner voice is waiting. Are you ready to listen?

Chapter Seven

The Nutrition-Confidence Connection You Never Knew Existed

Your Gut's Mental Influence

You've probably heard the saying "trust your gut," but did you know that your gut might actually be influencing your thoughts and feelings more than you realize? It turns out that what's going on in your belly can have a big impact on what's happening in your head.

Let's talk about something called the gut-brain axis. Don't worry; it's not as complicated as it sounds. Think of it like a two-way street between your digestive system and your brain. They're constantly chatting with each other, sharing information that affects how you feel, think, and even see yourself.

Here's the cool part: the tiny bacteria living in your gut (don't worry, they're the good kind) are like little factories pumping out important chemicals called neurotransmitters.

These are the same chemicals your brain uses to control your mood and thoughts. So, in a way, your gut is helping to run the show upstairs!

But it's not all sunshine and roses. When things go wrong in your gut, it can mess with your head, too. Ever had a stomachache and felt kind of foggy or cranky? That's because inflammation in your gut can lead to what we call "brain fog" and even make you feel down in the dumps.

And get this - if you're dealing with ongoing tummy troubles, it might be affecting how you feel about yourself and how you act around others. It's hard to feel confident and outgoing when you're worried about running to the bathroom or feeling bloated all the time.

Let's look at Diane's story to see how this all plays out in real life:

Diane was a 28-year-old marketing executive who loved her job but hated team meetings. Why? Because she was constantly dealing with IBS (Irritable Bowel Syndrome) and social anxiety.

- She'd skip lunch to avoid stomach issues during afternoon meetings.

- She'd panic about potential embarrassing "gut moments" in front of colleagues.

- Her confidence was at an all-time low, affecting her work performance.

Diane felt stuck and frustrated. She tried everything from meditation apps to speaking with a therapist, but nothing seemed to help. Then, she stumbled upon an article about the gut-brain connection.

Intrigued, Diane decided to give it a shot. She started small:

1. She cut back on processed foods and added more whole, plant-based options to her diet.

2. She began taking a daily probiotic supplement to support her gut bacteria.

3. She experimented with fermented foods like yogurt and kimchi.

4. She started practicing deep breathing exercises before meals to help with digestion.

At first, the changes felt overwhelming. However, as weeks turned into months, Diane noticed something amazing happening. Her stomach issues began to improve, and with that came a boost in her mood and energy levels.

The constant worry about bathroom emergencies started to fade. She felt more present in meetings, able to focus on the discussion instead of her churning stomach. As her gut health improved, so did her confidence.

Six months into her gut-health journey, Diane's colleagues noticed a change. "You seem different," her boss remarked after a presentation. "More sure of yourself." Diane smiled, knowing that the change went far beyond just feeling more confident; she felt like herself again.

Now, you might be thinking, "That's great for Diane, but what does it mean for me?" there are some general steps we can all take to support our gut health and potentially boost our confidence:

1. Eat a diverse diet rich in whole foods. Your gut bacteria love variety!

2. Consider adding fermented foods to your meals. Things like yogurt, kefir, and sauerkraut can be great for your gut.

3. Stay hydrated. Water helps keep things moving smoothly in your digestive system.

4. Manage stress. Remember that two-way street we talked about? Stress can affect your gut, too.

5. Get moving. Regular exercise is good for your whole body, including your digestive system.

It's important to remember that improving your gut health isn't a magic fix for all your problems. But it can be a powerful tool in your confidence-building toolkit.

Think about it: when you feel good physically, it's easier to feel good mentally. When you're not constantly worried about stomach issues, you have more mental energy to focus on other things, like crushing that presentation at work or enjoying time with friends.

The gut-brain connection is a fascinating area of research, and scientists are discovering new things about it all the time. While we still have a lot to learn, one thing is clear: taking care of your gut health can have benefits that reach far beyond your digestive system.

So, the next time you're feeling down or struggling with confidence, consider looking to your gut for some answers. It might just be the key to unlocking a more confident, happier you.

However, if you're dealing with serious digestive issues or mental health concerns, it's always best to talk to a healthcare professional. They can help you develop a plan that's tailored to your specific needs and situation.

In the end, the relationship between your gut and your brain is just one piece of the confidence puzzle. But it's an important piece and one that's often overlooked. By paying attention to this connection and taking steps to support your gut health, you might just find that you're nurturing your confidence from the inside out.

So go ahead, trust your gut. It might have more to say than you think!

Unexpected Happiness Bites

You've probably heard the saying, "You are what you eat," but did you know that what you eat can actually affect how you feel about yourself? It's true! Certain foods can give your brain a boost, making you feel happier and more confident. Let's discuss some of these unexpected happiness bites and see how they can transform your day.

First up, let's talk about omega-3 fatty acids. These little guys are like superheroes for your brain. They help reduce anxiety and keep your mood stable. Where can you find them? Think of foods like salmon, walnuts, and flaxseeds. Adding these to your diet might just help you feel a bit calmer and more in control.

Next on our list are probiotic-rich foods. Remember how we talked about the gut-brain connection? Which in turn can help stabilize your mood. Foods like yogurt, kefir, and sauerkraut are great sources of probiotics.

And here's a tasty surprise: dark chocolate can actually boost your mood! It contains compounds that can increase serotonin levels in your brain. Serotonin is often called the "feel-good" chemical because it can help improve your mood and make you feel more confident.

Now, let's see how incorporating these foods into your day can make a real difference. Meet Chris, a 35-year-old graphic designer who's been feeling a bit down lately.

Chris's Day of Happiness Bites:

7:00 AM: Chris wakes up feeling groggy and unenthusiastic about the day ahead. He drags himself to the kitchen, where he decides to try something new. Instead of his usual sugary cereal, he makes a bowl of Greek yogurt topped with walnuts and a drizzle of honey. The creamy yogurt provides a dose of probiotics, while the walnuts offer omega-3s.

As he eats, Chris notices that he feels more alert than usual. The combination of protein and healthy fats gives him a steady energy boost, unlike the sugar rush and crash he typically experiences.

10:00 AM: At work, Chris faces a challenging project. Normally, this would make him anxious, but today, he feels surprisingly calm. Could it be the omega-3s from breakfast kicking in? He takes a deep breath and dives into the task with a clear mind.

12:30 PM: Lunchtime rolls around, and Chris decides to continue his healthy eating experiment. He orders a salmon salad from the café downstairs. The salmon is rich in omega-3s, and the leafy greens provide additional nutrients that support brain health.

As he eats, Chris realizes he's feeling more positive about his work. The project that seemed daunting earlier now feels manageable. He even finds himself smiling as he chats with a coworker.

3:00 PM: The afternoon slump hits, and Chris is tempted to grab a candy bar from the vending machine. But remembering what he learned about dark chocolate, he opts for a small square of 70% dark chocolate instead. The rich flavor satisfies his craving, and he feels a subtle lift in his mood.

6:00 PM: After work, Chris usually feels too tired to socialize. But today, he agrees to meet a friend for dinner. They go to a Korean restaurant, where Chris tries kimchi for the first time. The fermented cabbage is tangy and delicious, and Chris learns it's also a great source of probiotics.

As they chat over dinner, Chris realizes he's feeling more engaged and confident in the conversation than he has in weeks. He even shares some ideas about a personal project he's been too insecure to talk about before.

9:00 PM: Back at home, Chris reflects on his day. He's surprised by how different he feels compared to his usual stressed and self-doubting self. Could these small changes in his diet really have made such a big difference?

Alex decides to keep experimenting with these "happiness bites" foods. He makes a grocery list for the week, including:

- Greek yogurt and kefir for probiotics

- Salmon and walnuts for omega-3s

- Dark leafy greens for overall brain health

- Dark chocolate for a mood-boosting treat

Over the next few weeks, Alex continues to incorporate these foods into his diet. He notices that his energy levels are more stable, his mood is generally more positive, and he feels more confident in his interactions at work and with friends.

Now, it's important to remember that food isn't a magic cure-all for mood and confidence issues. If you're dealing with serious anxiety or depression, it's crucial to talk to a healthcare professional. But for many of us, making small changes to our diet can have a surprisingly big impact on how we feel.

So, how can you start incorporating these happiness bites into your own life? Here are some simple ideas:

1. Start your day with a probiotic-rich breakfast. Try a yogurt parfait with berries and walnuts.

2. Add some omega-3-rich foods to your lunch. A salmon salad or a handful of walnuts on your usual sandwich can do the trick.

3. Keep some dark chocolate on hand for an afternoon mood boost. A little goes a long way!

4. Experiment with fermented foods like kimchi or sauerkraut. They can add a flavorful punch to your meals while supporting your gut health.

5. Stay hydrated! While not a food, drinking enough water is crucial for overall brain function and mood.

Remember, the goal isn't to completely overhaul your diet overnight. Small, consistent changes can add up to big results over time. And the best part? These foods aren't just good for your mood; they're delicious too!

As you start to pay more attention to how different foods make you feel, you might be surprised at the connections you discover. Maybe you'll notice that you feel more confident on days when you eat a protein-rich breakfast or that you handle stress better when you've had your omega-3s.

By tuning into these connections, you're not just improving your diet; you're giving yourself powerful tools to manage your mood and boost your confidence. And that's something worth celebrating, perhaps with a small square of dark chocolate!

So, the next time you're feeling down or lacking confidence, take a look at your plate. The solution to feeling better might just be a bite away.

Unmasking the Hunger Behind Self-Doubt

Have you ever felt like you're just not good enough, no matter how hard you try? Like there's a little voice in your head constantly telling you that you can't do it? It can show up as self-doubt and low confidence.

Let's look at three key nutrients that play a big role in how we feel about ourselves:

1. Vitamin D: The Sunshine Vitamin

Vitamin D is often called the "sunshine vitamin" because our bodies make it when our skin is exposed to sunlight. But did you know that not getting enough vitamin D can actually make you feel depressed?

Many people don't get enough vitamin D, especially if they live in places without much sunlight or spend a lot of time indoors. When you're low on vitamin D, you might feel sad, tired, and not very confident.

2. Iron: The Energy Maker

Iron is super important for our bodies. It helps carry oxygen to all our cells, including the ones in our brains. When we don't have enough iron, we can feel really tired and have trouble making decisions.

If you're always feeling worn out and can't seem to make up your mind about things, it might be worth checking your iron levels. This is especially true for women, vegetarians, and vegans, who are more likely to have low iron.

3. B Vitamins: The Stress Busters

B vitamins are like a team of superheroes for your brain. They help your body manage stress and keep your brain working well. When you don't get enough B vitamins, you might feel more stressed out and have trouble thinking clearly.

Foods like whole grains, eggs, and leafy green vegetables are great sources of B vitamins. If you're feeling stressed and foggy-headed a lot, you might not be getting enough of these important nutrients.

Now, let's look at how addressing these nutritional deficiencies can make a real difference in someone's life. Meet Maria, a 42-year-old teacher who had been struggling with self-doubt and low energy for years.

Maria's Story:

Maria loved her job teaching high school English, but lately, she'd been feeling like she just couldn't keep up. She was always tired, had trouble making decisions, and felt like she wasn't good enough, no matter how hard she tried.

She thought maybe she was just getting older or burning out. But then a friend suggested she talk to a doctor about her diet. Here's what happened:

- The doctor ran some tests and found that Maria was low in vitamin D, iron, and several B vitamins.

- Maria started taking supplements and made some changes to her diet. She added more leafy greens, eggs, and whole grains to her meals. She also started spending 15 minutes outside in the sun each day.

- At first, Maria didn't notice much difference. But after a few weeks, she realized she had more energy. She wasn't dragging herself through the day anymore.

- About a month later, Maria noticed something else: she was feeling more confident at work. She was coming up with new ideas for her lessons and actually sharing them with her colleagues.

- Two months after starting her new nutrition plan, Maria volunteered to lead a workshop at a teachers' conference - something she never would have had the confidence to do before.

- By the three-month mark, Maria's friends and family were commenting on how much happier and more confident she seemed. Maria realized that she felt like herself again - or maybe even a better version of herself than she'd ever known.

Maria's story shows us how powerful addressing nutritional deficiencies can be. But how can you tell if you might be dealing with something similar? Here are some signs to watch out for:

1. Constant fatigue, even after a good night's sleep

2. Difficulty making decisions or concentrating

3. Feeling sad or down for no apparent reason

4. Frequent headaches or dizziness

5. Pale skin or brittle nails

6. Feeling irritable or easily stressed

If you're experiencing these symptoms, it might be worth talking to a doctor about your diet and getting some blood tests done. But even if you're not showing these signs, paying attention to your nutrition can still help boost your confidence and overall well-being.

So, what can you do to make sure you're getting the nutrients you need? Here are some simple steps:

1. Eat a varied diet with lots of different fruits and vegetables. Different colors often mean different nutrients, so aim for a rainbow on your plate.

2. Include good sources of iron in your meals, like lean meats, beans, and leafy greens. If you don't eat meat, pair iron-rich plant foods with vitamin C-rich foods to help your body absorb the iron better.

3. Consider a vitamin D supplement, especially if you live in a place without much sunlight. You can also get vitamin D from fatty fish, egg yolks, and fortified foods.

4. Don't skimp on whole grains, which are great sources of B vitamins. Things like brown rice, whole wheat bread, and oatmeal are all good choices.

5. If you're concerned about deficiencies, talk to your doctor. They might recommend blood tests or supplements.

Changing your diet isn't about being perfect. It's about making small, consistent changes that add up over time. You don't have to overhaul your entire diet overnight. Start with one or two changes and build from there.

As you start paying more attention to your nutrition, you might be surprised at how it affects not just your physical health but your mental and emotional well-being, too. That little voice of self-doubt might start to get quieter, replaced by a growing sense of confidence and capability.

So, the next time you're feeling down on yourself or struggling with self-doubt, take a moment to consider what you've been eating. Your body might be trying to tell you something important. By listening to it and giving it the nutrients it needs, you might just find the confidence you've been looking for was inside you all along; it just needed the right fuel to shine through.

Food for Inner Strength

Ever noticed how your mood can swing wildly throughout the day? One minute, you're on top of the world; the next, you're doubting every decision you've ever made. If you choose the right food, the food you eat can give you consistent energy and a more confident you.

First things first: regular, balanced meals are key for mood stability. When you skip meals or rely on quick, sugary snacks, your blood sugar goes on a wild ride. And guess what? Your mood follows right along. You might feel great for a little while after that candy bar, but when the sugar crash hits, so does the self-doubt and irritability.

So, what does a balanced meal look like? Think of it as a team effort:

- Protein: This is your mood stabilizer. It helps keep your blood sugar steady and provides the building blocks for feel-good brain chemicals.

- Complex carbs: These are your energy providers. They give you a steady stream of fuel, unlike the quick spike and crash from simple sugars.

- Healthy fats: These are your brain boosters. They help your body absorb certain vitamins and are crucial for brain health.

- Fruits and veggies: These are your nutrient powerhouses. They're packed with vitamins and minerals that support overall health and well-being.

Now, let's talk about how to sneak some mood-boosting foods into your daily meals. Remember those omega-3s and probiotics we talked about earlier? Here are some easy ways to include them:

- Breakfast: Try a yogurt parfait with berries and walnuts. You get probiotics from the yogurt, omega-3s from the walnuts, and a host of other nutrients from the berries.

- Lunch: How about a salmon salad on whole grain bread? You've got omega-3s from the salmon, complex carbs from the bread, and a variety of nutrients from the veggies in your salad.

- Dinner: Stir-fry some tofu with a variety of colorful veggies and serve it over brown rice. Top it with a sprinkle of pumpkin seeds for an extra omega-3 boost.

- Snacks: Keep some dark chocolate and mixed nuts on hand for a quick mood-boosting snack.

Don't forget about hydration! Your brain is about 75% water, and even mild dehydration can affect your mood and cognitive function. Aim to drink water throughout the day. If you find plain water boring, try infusing it with fruits or herbs for a flavor boost.

Now, let's look at how putting all this into practice can make a real difference. Meet Tom, a 38-year-old software developer who struggled with erratic eating habits and mood swings.

Tom's Story:

Tom was known in his office for two things: his brilliant coding skills and his unpredictable moods. Some days, he'd be full of energy and ideas; other days, he'd be irritable and doubt every line of code he wrote.

Tom's typical day looked like this:

- Skip breakfast because he was running late

- Grab a large coffee and a muffin mid-morning when hunger hit

- Work through lunch, maybe grabbing a candy bar from the vending machine

- Order takeout for dinner, often eating late at night

Tom decided to try a new approach. Here's what he did:

Week 1: Tom started by simply eating three meals a day at regular times. He didn't worry too much about what he was eating yet; he just focused on the timing.

Week 2: Tom began planning his meals in advance. He stocked his fridge with easy-to-prepare foods like pre-washed salad greens, rotisserie chicken, and whole-grain bread.

Week 3: Tom started incorporating more mood-boosting foods into his meals. He added walnuts to his morning oatmeal, switched to salmon for some of his lunches, and kept dark chocolate on hand for an afternoon snack.

Week 4: Tom began paying attention to how different foods made him feel. He noticed that he felt more alert and positive on days when he ate a protein-rich breakfast.

After a month of his new eating habits, Tom noticed some big changes:

- His energy levels were more consistent throughout the day

- He felt more confident in meetings and was able to express his ideas clearly

- His mood swings had decreased significantly

- He was sleeping better at night

- He even got a compliment from his boss about his improved performance

Tom's story shows us how powerful strategic meal planning can be. But remember, it's not about being perfect. It's about making small, consistent changes that add up over time.

Here's a quick recap of the key points we've covered:

1. The gut-brain connection plays a big role in how we feel and think about ourselves

2. Certain foods can boost our mood and confidence through their nutrient profiles

3. Nutritional deficiencies can show up as self-doubt and low confidence

4. Strategic meal planning helps support emotional resilience and consistent energy levels

So, what can you do to start harnessing the power of food for inner strength? Here are some action steps to get you started:

1. Keep a food-mood journal for two weeks. Write down what you eat and how you feel afterward. You might spot some interesting connections!

2. Try to include at least one probiotic-rich food in your diet each day. This could be yogurt, kefir, sauerkraut, or any other fermented food you enjoy.

3. Schedule a check-up with your doctor to test for common nutritional deficiencies. Knowing where you stand can help you make targeted improvements.

4. Create a weekly meal plan that includes a variety of mood-boosting foods. Don't worry about making it perfect - even planning just a few meals a week is a great start.

As we've seen, nourishing your body plays a crucial role in building confidence from the inside out. But confidence isn't just about what's happening internally—it's also about how you present yourself to the world. In our next chapter, we'll explore how you can set boundaries that allow you to be kind but firm and how to set limits.

You are what you eat - so why not eat your way to a more confident you?

Chapter Eight

Boundary Alchemy: Turning No into Your Greatest Yes

The Unexpected Key to Freedom

Picture this: You're standing at the edge of a vast, open field. The grass stretches as far as the eye can see, and you feel a sense of limitless possibility. But here's the twist - without any fences or markers, you're not sure where to go or what to do. You might wander aimlessly, feeling overwhelmed by the sheer expanse of options.

Now, imagine that same field with a clear path running through it. Suddenly, you have direction. You can see where you're going, and you feel a sense of purpose. This is exactly what boundaries do for our lives.

Boundaries aren't walls that shut us in. They're guideposts that show us the way.

Let's break this down:

1. Boundaries protect your time and energy, allowing you to focus on what truly matters

Think of your time and energy like a garden. Without fences, anyone can trample through, picking your flowers and stomping on your veggies. But with a nice, sturdy fence, you get to decide what (and who) comes in.

Abigail, a marketing whiz we'll meet in a bit, used to say "yes" to every project that came her way. She'd work late into the night, answer emails on weekends, and even skip lunch to squeeze in "just one more task." Sound familiar?

Her garden was a mess. Weeds (unnecessary tasks) were choking out the flowers (important projects). She was exhausted, cranky, and nowhere near as productive as she thought she should be.

Then, Abigail learned about boundaries. She started small:

- No checking emails after 7 PM

- Lunch break away from her desk every day

- One "no" per week to non-essential requests

At first, it felt weird. She worried people would think she was slacking off. But here's what really happened:

- Her work got better because she was more focused

- She had more energy for creative thinking

- She actually finished projects faster

By protecting her time and energy with boundaries, Abigail created space for what really mattered. Her garden started to bloom.

2. Clear boundaries in relationships foster mutual respect and understanding

Now, let's talk about the people in your life. Relationships without boundaries are like playing a game without rules. It's confusing and frustrating, and someone always ends up feeling cheated.

Clear boundaries are like a good, solid handshake. They say, "I respect you, and I respect myself."

Here's what that looks like:

- Telling your friend you need a night to yourself instead of making up an excuse

- Letting your partner know when you need space to process your emotions

- Telling your coworker you can't take on their project because you're at capacity

When you set clear boundaries, you're actually giving people a map of your needs and limits. It's not selfish; it's helpful!

3. Saying "no" to less important commitments opens doors to greater opportunities

This is where the magic happens. When you start saying "no" to things that don't align with your goals or values, you create space for amazing opportunities to show up.

It's like cleaning out your closet. You get rid of the clothes you never wear, and suddenly, you have room for that perfect jacket you've been eyeing.

Some ways to practice this:

- Say no to after-work drinks if you're trying to start a side business

- Decline a committee position that doesn't excite you

- Turn down a "good" opportunity to leave room for a great one

Every "no" is really a "yes" to something else. Something better.

Now, let's meet Kendra and see how this played out in real life.

***

Kendra was the go-to person in her marketing firm. Need a last-minute presentation? Kendra's on it. Client emergency at 5 PM on a Friday? Kendra to the rescue!

She thought being available 24/7 made her invaluable. In reality, she was burning out fast.

One day, after missing her son's school play for a non-urgent work task, Kendra realized something had to change. She started setting boundaries:

1. She defined her work hours and stuck to them

2. She prioritized tasks and learned to say "no" to low-priority requests

3. She stopped answering work emails on weekends

At first, Kendra was terrified. She was sure she'd be seen as lazy or uncommitted. But something surprising happened.

Her work got better. Way better.

With clear boundaries, Kendra could focus deeply on important projects. She started producing higher-quality work in less time. Her stress levels dropped, and her creativity soared.

Her boss noticed. Instead of seeing Kendra as less committed, he saw her as more professional and efficient. Six months after Kendra started setting boundaries, she was offered a promotion to team lead.

What brought about this promotion? Part of why she got the promotion was her ability to manage her time and energy effectively, skills she developed by setting boundaries.

Kendra's story shows us that boundaries aren't just good for us personally - they can catapult our professional lives, too.

So, how can you start your own boundary revolution? Here are some steps:

1. Identify your limits: What makes you feel stressed, resentful, or overwhelmed?

2. Start small: Choose one area to set a boundary in

3. Communicate clearly: Let others know about your new boundary

4. Stick to it: Boundaries only work if you enforce them

5. Adjust as needed: It's okay to tweak your boundaries over time

Remember, setting boundaries isn't about building walls. It's about creating a safe, nurturing space where you can grow and thrive. It's about turning your "no" into the biggest, most powerful "yes" to yourself and your dreams.

Kindness Meets Backbone in Communication

Let's discuss the art of setting boundaries with both kindness and backbone. It's like being a friendly bouncer at the club of your life; you're not there to be mean, but you've got a job to do.

Effective boundary-setting is all about clear, kind communication. It's finding that sweet spot between being a doormat and being a jerk. You want to stand up for yourself without stepping on others. Sounds tricky, right? Don't worry; we've got some tricks up our sleeve.

First up, let's talk about "I" statements. These are your secret weapon in boundary-setting.

Instead of saying, "You're always interrupting me!" try, "I feel frustrated when I'm interrupted because it breaks my concentration."

See the difference? You're not pointing fingers. You're just saying how you feel and why. It's like magic; people are way less likely to get defensive when you talk this way.

Here's a quick formula for "I" statements:

"I feel *** when *** because ***."

Easy, right? Give it a try next time you need to set a boundary. You might be surprised at how well it works.

Now, let's tackle the next piece of the puzzle: acknowledging the other person's perspective.

This is where empathy comes in. You want to show that you understand where they're coming from, even if you don't agree. It's like saying, "I hear you, but here's where I stand."

For example: "I understand you need this report urgently, and I know it's important. However, I've already committed to finishing another project by the end of the day."

You're not budging on your boundary, but you're showing that you get their side, too. It's a bit like a verbal hug before you say no.

Finally, let's talk about offering alternatives or compromises. This is where you can get creative.

Sometimes, you can find a win-win solution that respects your boundaries and still helps the other person. It's not always possible, and that's okay. But when you can do it, it's pretty awesome.

For instance: "I can't take on the whole project, but I could help you brainstorm ideas for an hour this afternoon."

You're still saying no to the big ask, but you're offering a smaller way to help. It's like serving a slice of cake instead of the whole cake - still sweet, just not too much.

Now, let's see how this all plays out in real life. We're going to do some role-play scenarios. Imagine these are happening to you:

Scenario 1: Your coworker always dumps last-minute work on you.

Coworker: "Hey, I know it's 4:30, but could you just quickly look over this 50-page report before you go? I need it first thing tomorrow."

You: "I understand this report is urgent for you, and I want to help. However, I have a commitment after work that I can't reschedule. I could look at the executive summary for 15 minutes now, or I could review the full report first thing tomorrow morning. Which would be more helpful?"

See what we did there? We used an "I" statement to explain your situation, acknowledged their need, and offered two alternatives that respect your boundaries.

Scenario 2: Your friend always vents to you about their problems, leaving you emotionally drained.

Friend: "Ugh, you won't believe what happened today! ***"

You: "I care about you and want to support you. At the same time, I've been feeling overwhelmed lately when our conversations focus heavily on problems. I wonder if we could spend the first 15 minutes catching up on your day, and then maybe we could do something fun together? I'd love to hear about the good stuff in your life, too."

Here, we've acknowledged the friend's need to vent, expressed your own feelings, and offered a compromise that allows for some venting but also protects your emotional energy.

Scenario 3: Your family member keeps asking to borrow money.

Family Member: "Hey, I'm a little short this month. Could you lend me $200? I'll pay you back soon, I promise."

You: "I know financial struggles can be really stressful, and I'm sorry you're in this situation. However, lending money has caused tension in our relationship before, and I'm not comfortable doing it anymore. Maybe we could look at your budget together and see if there are any areas where you could cut back?"

In this case, we've shown empathy for their situation, clearly stated the boundary, and offered an alternative way to help that doesn't involve lending money.

These scenarios show how you can blend kindness with firmness. It's not about being harsh or cold - it's about being clear and respectful, both to yourself and others.

Setting boundaries is a skill. Like any skill, it takes practice. You might fumble a bit at first, and that's okay. Keep at it. Each time you set a boundary, you're building your "boundary muscle."

Here's a quick recap of our boundary-setting formula:

1. Use "I" statements to express your needs

2. Acknowledge the other person's perspective

3. Offer alternatives or compromises when possible (but don't compromise your core boundaries)

Think of it like a boundary-setting sandwich. The "I" statement and the acknowledgment are the bread, and the alternative or compromise (if appropriate) is the filling.

As you practice this, you'll find your own style. Maybe you'll add a dash of humor or a sprinkle of storytelling. That's great! The key is to find a way that feels authentic to you.

Setting boundaries isn't about building walls. It's about creating healthy spaces where relationships can flourish. It's about saying "yes" to yourself so you can give your best "yes" to others.

So go ahead, flex those boundary muscles. Your future self will thank you for it.

Your Secret Fuel for Success

Let's talk about your secret fuel for success. It's not some fancy energy drink or a magic pill. It's something you already have inside you: your ability to set boundaries. Think of boundaries as your personal energy shield, protecting you from the stuff that drains you and letting in the good stuff that powers you up.

Imagine you're a car. Your energy is your fuel. Without boundaries, you're like a car with holes in the gas tank. You keep filling up, but the fuel leaks out before you can use it. But with strong boundaries? Your tank stays full, and you can go the distance.

Let's break this down and see how it works.

First up, we need to spot the sneaky time-wasters and energy drains in your life. These are the holes in your gas tank.

Take a minute and think about your day. What makes you feel tired or frustrated? Maybe it's that coworker who always wants to chat when you're trying to focus. Or those hours you spend scrolling on your phone before bed. These are your energy leaks.

Here's a quick way to find them:

1. For a week, jot down what you do each day.

2. At the end of each day, mark activities that made you feel energized or productive.

3. Mark activities that left you feeling drained or like you wasted time.

You might be surprised at what you find. Maybe that "quick" social media check is eating up hours of your day. Or those late-night Netflix binges are making your mornings harder.

Once you spot these leaks, you can start to plug them. That's where boundaries come in.

Next, let's talk about setting up routines and systems to protect your best hours.

Think about when you're at your best. Are you a morning person, firing on all cylinders at 6 AM? Or do you hit your stride in the afternoon?

These are your golden hours. They're when your brain is sharpest, and your energy is highest. Protecting these hours is like putting a forcefield around your most valuable resource.

Here's how you might do it:

- If you're a morning person, set a boundary of no meetings before 10 AM. Use those early hours for your most important work.

- If you're an afternoon person, block off 2-4 PM for focused work. No interruptions are allowed.

Creating these boundaries might feel weird at first. People might push back. But stick with it. You're protecting your most valuable asset: your best energy and focus.

Now, let's tackle the art of saying "no" and delegating.

This is where a lot of people struggle. We want to be helpful and to be seen as team players. But here's the truth: saying yes to everything means saying no to your own priorities.

Think of it this way: every time you say yes to something, you're saying no to something else. Maybe you're saying no to family time, or to working on that big project, or even to getting enough sleep.

So, how do you decide what to say no to? Ask yourself:

- Does this align with my long-term goals?

- Is this the best use of my time and energy?

- If I say yes to this, what am I saying no to?

If the answer to these questions isn't a clear "yes," it might be time to say no or delegate.

Delegating isn't about dumping work on others. It's about matching tasks to the right people. Maybe your coworker loves the kind of task you find draining. Delegating to them could be a win-win.

Now, let's see how this all comes together in real life. Meet Kevin.

Kevin was a classic overachiever. Always the first to volunteer for projects, always staying late at the office. He prided himself on being the go-to guy. But inside, he was burning out fast.

His days were a blur of meetings; his nights were spent catching up on email. His big dreams? They were gathering dust while he ran on the hamster wheel of busyness.

One day, after missing his kid's school play for the third time, Kevin realized something had to change. He started setting boundaries.

First, he looked for his energy drains. He realized those "quick" coffee chats with coworkers often stretched into hour-long gab sessions. And he was spending hours each night responding to non-urgent emails.

Next, he protected his golden hours. Kevin was a morning person, so he set a boundary: no meetings before 10 AM. He used those early hours for his most important work.

Finally, he learned to say no and delegate. He stopped volunteering for every project. Instead, he focused on the ones that aligned with his long-term career goals. He delegated tasks that others could do, freeing up his time for high-impact work.

At first, it was hard. Kevin worried people would think he wasn't a team player. But something amazing happened.

His work got better. Way better. With clear boundaries, Kevin could focus deeply on important projects. He started producing higher-quality work in less time.

His stress levels dropped. He had energy left at the end of the day for his family and his personal goals. He even started that side project he'd been dreaming about for years.

And his boss? Instead of being disappointed, she was impressed. She saw Kevin as more professional and more strategic. Six months after Kevin started setting boundaries, he was offered a promotion.

Kevin's story shows us that boundaries aren't just good for us personally - they can rocket-boost our careers, too.

So, how can you start your own boundary revolution? Here are some steps:

1. Track your time and energy for a week. Spot those leaks.

2. Identify your golden hours. Build a fortress around them.

3. Practice saying no. Start small, with low-stakes situations.

4. Look for tasks you can delegate. It's not about dumping work - it's about smart allocation.

5. Communicate your boundaries clearly and kindly.

Remember, setting boundaries isn't about building walls. It's about creating a safe, energizing space where you can thrive. It's about turning your "no" into fuel for your biggest "yes" - to your goals, your dreams, your best life.

Your boundaries are your secret weapon. They're the invisible force that keeps your energy tank full, your focus sharp, and your path clear. So go ahead, draw those lines. Your future self will thank you for it.

Embrace Limits, Empower Your Self-Worth

Let's think about the transformative power of boundaries and how they can supercharge your self-worth. Picture boundaries as a cozy sweater that keeps you warm and comfortable, not a straitjacket that holds you back. They're your personal cheerleader, always rooting for your well-being.

First up, let's flip the script on "no." Most of us grow up thinking "no" is a bad word. But here's the truth bomb: every "no" is actually a big, beautiful "yes" to something else.

When you say no to staying late at work, you're saying yes to family time. When you say no to that extra slice of cake, you're saying yes to feeling energized tomorrow. See how that works?

Try this: Next time you need to say no, add a silent "because" after it. "No, I can't take on that project. . .because I'm prioritizing my mental health." It's not just a no; it's an affirmation of what matters to you.

Here's a quick exercise:

1. Write down three things you often say yes to, even though you don't want to.

2. Now, write what you're actually saying yes to by saying no to these things.

3. Practice saying these new "yes" statements out loud.

Feels good, right? That's the power of reframing.

Now, let's talk about celebrating your boundary-setting wins. Even tiny ones.

Did you turn down a non-urgent request to focus on your priorities? That's a win! Did you ask for help instead of overloading yourself? Winner winner, chicken dinner!

These might seem small, but they're huge steps towards a more empowered you. It's like working out; each rep builds your boundary muscle.

Try keeping a "boundary win" journal. At the end of each day, write down one boundary you set or maintained. It could be as simple as "I took a lunch break away from my desk." Over time, you'll see how these small wins add up to big changes.

Next up: using boundaries as a tool for personal growth and self-discovery.

Setting boundaries isn't just about saying no; it's about figuring out what you want to say yes to. It's a journey of self-discovery.

Each time you set a boundary, ask yourself:

- What does this boundary protect?

- What does it make space for?

- What does it tell me about my values and priorities?

You might be surprised at what you learn about yourself.

For example, if you set a boundary around not checking work emails after 7 PM, you might discover that you value work-life balance more than you realized. Or if you start saying no to social events that drain you, you might learn that you're more introverted than you thought.

These insights are gold. They help you align your life more closely with who you really are.

Now, let's meet Sally and see how this played out in real life.

Sally was the office pushover. Need someone to cover a shift? Sally's your gal. Last-minute project? Sally will stay late. She thought being agreeable made her a good person. But inside, she was drowning in resentment and self-doubt.

One day, after crying in the bathroom for the third time that week, Sally decided enough was enough. She started setting boundaries.

At first, it was terrifying. She worried people would hate her. But she started small:

- She declined a non-urgent meeting to finish an important report.

- She asked a coworker to help with a project instead of doing it all herself.

- She left work on time to attend her painting class.

Each small win built her confidence. She started seeing "no" as a positive thing - a way to say yes to her own needs and goals.

As she set more boundaries, Sally started to discover things about herself. She realized she loved strategic work but disliked administrative tasks. She found out she was more creative when she had downtime.

These insights helped her reshape her role at work. She started delegating admin tasks and took on more strategic projects. Her work improved, and she felt more fulfilled.

The biggest surprise? People respected her more, not less. Her boss saw her as more professional and confident. Six months after Sally started setting boundaries, she was offered a leadership position.

Sally's story shows us that boundaries aren't just about saying no - they're about saying yes to your best self.

Let's recap the key points:

1. Setting boundaries creates space for personal growth and empowerment. It's like clearing the clutter from your life so you can see what really matters.

2. Effective boundary-setting involves clear, compassionate communication. It's not about being mean; it's about being clear and kind.

3. Well-defined boundaries help allocate time and energy towards meaningful goals. They're your personal bodyguards, protecting your most valuable resources.

4. Viewing boundaries positively can boost confidence and self-worth. Each boundary you set is a vote of confidence in yourself.

Ready to start your boundary revolution? Here are some action steps:

1. Identify one area in your life where you need stronger boundaries. Maybe it's work, relationships, or how you spend your free time.

2. Practice crafting assertive yet kind responses to boundary-crossing situations. Remember the "I feel... when... because..." formula we learned earlier.

3. Create a daily routine that protects your most productive hours. Build a fortress around your golden time.

4. Reflect on how setting a boundary made you feel more empowered and use this as motivation. Each win, no matter how small, is fuel for your journey.

As we wrap up this chapter, think about how far you've come. You've learned to set boundaries, to say no to what doesn't serve you, and to protect your time and energy. You're no longer a leaf blown about by other people's demands; you're the author of your own story.

But this is just the beginning. Now that you've cleared the clutter and created space in your life, it's time to fill that space with your dreams and aspirations.

In our next chapter, "Your Personal Board of Directors: Curating Your Inner Circle," you'll learn about relationships, mentors for success, having a tribe of allies, and ways to boost your confidence.

Chapter Nine

Your Personal Board of Directors: Curating Your Inner Circle

Relationships That Erode Confidence

We've all heard the saying, "You are the average of the five people you spend the most time with." While this might sound like an oversimplification, there's a kernel of truth in it. The people we surround ourselves with have a profound impact on our mindset, our actions, and ultimately, our success.

But what happens when those relationships aren't helping us grow? What if, instead of lifting us up, they're slowly chipping away at our confidence?

Let's look closely at the world of toxic relationships and how they can secretly sabotage our self-esteem and personal growth.

Signs of Toxic Relationships

Toxic relationships come in many forms, but they all share one thing in common: they leave you feeling drained, doubting yourself, or stuck in a negative headspace. Here are some red flags to watch out for:

- Constant criticism: Does someone in your life always seem to find fault with you?

- Manipulation: Do you often feel guilted into doing things you don't want to do?

- Lack of support: When you share your dreams, are you met with eye rolls or discouragement?

- Energy vampire: Do you feel exhausted after spending time with this person?

- One-sided effort: Are you always the one reaching out or making compromises?

If you nodded along to any of these, you might be dealing with a toxic relationship. But don't worry; recognizing it is the first step towards change.

The Confidence Crusher

Now, you might be thinking, "Sure, these relationships aren't great, but how bad can they really be?"

The answer? Pretty darn bad.

Toxic relationships are like slow-acting poison for your self-esteem. They seep into your thoughts, making you question your worth and abilities. Over time, this constant negativity can lead to:

- Decreased self-confidence

- Increased anxiety and stress

- Difficulty making decisions

- Lowered motivation and ambition

- A tendency to settle for less than you deserve

Think about it. If you're constantly surrounded by people who doubt you or put you down, it's only natural that you might start to believe them. You might find yourself playing small, avoiding risks, or giving up on your dreams altogether.

But here's the good news: it doesn't have to be this way.

Breaking Free: Strategies for Healthier Relationships

So, how do we break free from these confidence-crushing relationships? It's not always easy, but it is possible. Here are some strategies to help you create a more supportive inner circle:

1. Set clear boundaries: It's okay to say no. It's okay to limit your time with people who drain you. Practice saying, "I'm not comfortable with that," or "That doesn't work for me."

2. Communicate your needs: Sometimes, people might not realize how their behavior affects you. Have an honest conversation about how you feel.

3. Seek out positive influences: Actively look for people who inspire and motivate you. Join clubs, attend events, or take classes related to your interests.

4. Practice self-care: your relationship with yourself is the most important one. Make time for activities that boost your confidence and make you feel good.

5. Consider professional help: If you're struggling to break free from a toxic relationship, don't hesitate to seek help from a therapist or counselor.

Remember, you deserve relationships that lift you up, not tear you down.

Sophia's Story: From Toxic Friendship to Thriving Career

Let's look at how this plays out in real life with Sophia's story.

Sophia was a talented graphic designer with big dreams of starting her own agency. But there was one problem: her best friend, Kate.

Whenever Sophia shared her aspirations, Kate would say things like, "Isn't that a bit risky?" or "Do you really think you can compete with the big agencies?" Over time, Sophia started to doubt herself. She passed up opportunities and stayed in a job she'd outgrown.

One day, Sophia attended a design conference and met Lisa, a successful agency owner. Unlike Kate, Lisa was excited about Sophia's ideas and offered encouragement and practical advice.

This contrast was eye-opening for Sophia. She realized how much Kate's negativity had been holding her back. It wasn't easy, but Sophia decided to distance herself from Kate and surround herself with more supportive people like Lisa.

The result? Within a year, Sophia had launched her own small agency and was thriving. She felt more confident, energized, and excited about her future than ever before.

Sophia's story shows us the power of our inner circle. By recognizing the toxic influence in her life and actively seeking out more positive relationships, she was able to transform her career and her confidence.

Your Turn: Curating Your Inner Circle

Now it's your turn. Take a moment to reflect on your relationships. Who makes you feel energized and inspired? Who leaves you feeling drained or doubtful?

It's not about cutting people out of your life entirely (unless that's necessary for your well-being). It's about being intentional about who you spend your time with and whose opinions you value.

Think of it like curating your own personal board of directors. You want people who believe in you, challenge you to grow, and support your dreams.

Remember, you have the power to shape your inner circle. By surrounding yourself with positive influences, you're not just boosting your confidence - you're setting yourself up for success in all areas of your life.

So, who's on your board?

Your Personal Success Mentors

Let's think about one of the most powerful tools you can use to boost your confidence and achieve your goals: Your Personal Success Mentors. This isn't about finding real-life mentors (though that's great, too!) It's about creating an imaginary advisory board of inspiring figures who can guide you through life's challenges.

Imagine having a group of the world's most successful and inspiring people on speed dial, ready to offer you advice whenever you need it. Sounds pretty awesome, right? Your board can include:

- Historical figures who've changed the world

- Modern-day leaders in business, politics, or social change

- Fictional characters who inspire you

- Personal heroes from your own life

The key is diversity. You want a range of perspectives and expertise. Maybe you'll have Marie Curie for her scientific brilliance, Michelle Obama for her grace under pressure, and your grandma for her practical wisdom.

Here's a tip: Aim for 5-7 board members. Too few, and you might miss out on diverse viewpoints. Too many, and it could get overwhelming.

Imagining Their Advice

Now comes the really cool part. When you're faced with a challenge or decision, you can "consult" your board. How would each of them approach the situation?

Let's say you're nervous about a job interview. You might imagine:

- Steve Jobs telling you to trust your instincts and think differently

- Maya Angelou reminding you of your inherent worth and unique voice

- Your favorite teacher encouraging you to prepare thoroughly and be yourself

The goal isn't to predict exactly what they'd say. It's about using their known qualities and approaches to gain new perspectives on your situation.

Challenging Your Limits

One of the best things about this imaginary board is how it can help you push past your self-imposed limits. When you're doubting yourself, your board members can be there to challenge those doubts.

Feeling like you can't start that business? Imagine what Oprah Winfrey might say about believing in yourself and taking risks. Worried you're too old to learn a new skill? Picture Betty White reminding you it's never too late to try something new.

Your board can be your personal cheer squad, pushing you to be your best self.

Mark's Story: Board Meetings in His Mind

Let's look at how this works in practice with Mark's story.

Mark was a young entrepreneur struggling to get his eco-friendly packaging company off the ground. He had a great idea, but he was facing challenges with funding, manufacturing, and self-doubt.

That's when Mark decided to create his own personal board of directors. His chosen mentors included:

- Elon Musk for innovative thinking

- Jane Goodall for environmental passion

- His former basketball coach for team leadership

- Walt Disney for creative problem-solving

- His grandmother for perseverance

Whenever Mark faced a hurdle, he'd hold a "board meeting" in his mind. He'd imagine sitting around a table with these inspirational figures, presenting his problem, and listening to their advice.

When Mark was struggling with a manufacturing issue, he imagined Elon Musk suggesting out-of-the-box solutions and reminding him that setbacks are part of the innovation process. Jane Goodall's voice in his head kept him focused on the environmental impact of his work, motivating him to push through difficulties.

During a particularly tough period when Mark was considering giving up, he imagined his grandmother telling him about the hardships she'd overcome in her life. This gave him the strength to keep going.

The advice Mark "received" wasn't always what he expected. Sometimes, it challenged his assumptions or pushed him out of his comfort zone. But that was the point - to gain new perspectives and push his boundaries.

Over time, Mark found himself becoming more confident in his decision-making. He started to internalize the wisdom of his imaginary mentors. When faced with a challenge, he'd ask himself, "What would Walt Disney do to make this more creative?" or "How would my coach approach building a stronger team?"

The result? Mark's company began to thrive. He credits his imaginary board with helping him overcome obstacles, stay true to his vision, and build the confidence to lead his growing team.

Creating Your Own Board

Now it's your turn to assemble your dream team of mentors. Here's how to get started:

1. Reflect on your goals and challenges. What areas of your life could use some guidance?

2. Think about people (real or fictional) who inspire you in those areas. Who has qualities or achievements you admire?

3. Choose a diverse group. Aim for a mix of backgrounds, skills, and perspectives.

4. Get to know your board members. Read their biographies, watch interviews, or study their work to understand their approaches and philosophies.

5. Start "consulting" your board. When faced with a decision or challenge, take a moment to imagine what advice each member might give.

This is your personal tool. There's no right or wrong way to do it. The important thing is that it works for you.

Your Evolving Board

As you grow and your goals change, don't be afraid to shake up your board. Maybe you'll "fire" some members and bring in new ones. That's totally okay. Your imaginary board should evolve with you.

The power of this technique lies in its ability to expand your thinking and boost your confidence. By "consulting" with these inspiring figures, you're reminding yourself of your potential and pushing yourself to think bigger.

So, who will you invite to your personal board of directors? The world's most inspiring minds are waiting to guide you; all you have to do is imagine.

Building Your Tribe of Allies and Guides

Let's talk about one of the most powerful ways to boost your confidence and achieve your goals: Building Your Tribe of Allies and Guides. This isn't just about having friends. It's about creating a network of people who support you, challenge you, and help you grow.

Think of it like this: You're the hero of your own story. But every hero needs a support team, right? That's what we're building here.

Finding Your Allies

First things first: Who's already in your corner? Look around at your existing network. You might be surprised by the potential mentors and supporters hiding in plain sight.

- That coworker who always has great advice? Potential mentor.

- Your friend who's killing it in their career? Could be a valuable ally.

- The relative who's overcome similar challenges to yours? They might have wisdom to share.

The key is to look beyond the obvious. Sometimes, our best supporters aren't the people we see every day. They might be acquaintances, old classmates, or even someone you admire from afar.

Make a list. Who inspires you? Who has skills or knowledge you'd like to learn? Who seems to have figured out something you're struggling with?

These are your potential tribe members.

Reaching Out: It's Not as Scary as You Think

Okay, so you've identified some potential mentors and allies. Now what? The idea of reaching out can feel pretty scary. What if they say no? What if you bother them?

Here's a secret: Most people love to help. It makes them feel good. And successful people? They often feel a responsibility to "pay it forward."

So take a deep breath and try these techniques:

1. Start small: Don't ask for a huge commitment right away. Maybe just ask for a quick coffee chat or a 15-minute phone call.

2. Be specific: Instead of asking, "Will you be my mentor?" try something like, "I really admire how you've built your business. Could I ask you a few questions about how you got started?"

3. Show your value: Mentorship isn't just about taking. How can you help them? Maybe you have skills they need or connections that could be useful.

4. Follow up: After your chat, send a thank-you note. Let them know how their advice helped you. People like to know they've made a difference.

The worst they can say is no. And if they do? No biggie. Move on to the next person on your list.

Creating Your Support Squad

While mentors are great, don't forget about your peers. These are the people in the trenches with you, facing similar challenges and celebrating similar victories.

Building a peer support group can be incredibly powerful. Here's how to get started:

- Identify your goals: What do you want to achieve? Find people with similar ambitions.

- Look for diversity: Don't just stick with people in your field. Different perspectives can lead to amazing insights.

- Set expectations: How often will you meet? What's the format? Make sure everyone's on the same page.

- Give as much as you take: Support is a two-way street. Be there for your peers as much as they're there for you.

- Celebrate wins: When someone in the group achieves something, make a big deal out of it. It lifts everyone up.

One great way to create this kind of support system is through a mastermind group. This brings us to Lisa's story...

Lisa's Mastermind Magic

Lisa was a freelance graphic designer. She was good at her job, but she felt stuck. She wanted to grow her business, but she wasn't sure how. And if she was being honest, she was scared to try.

Then, a friend invited her to join a mastermind group. Lisa was hesitant at first. What could she offer? But she decided to give it a shot.

The group met every two weeks. There were six members, all running different types of small businesses. At each meeting, they'd take turns sharing their challenges and brainstorming solutions.

At first, Lisa mostly listened. But soon, she started to open up. She shared her dream of landing bigger clients and maybe even starting her own agency someday.

To her surprise, the group didn't laugh or tell her she was dreaming too big. Instead, they got excited. They started throwing out ideas:

"Have you thought about partnering with a web developer to offer more comprehensive services?"

"I know someone who runs a marketing agency. Want me to introduce you?"

"Why don't you create a case study of your best project to showcase what you can do?"

Lisa left that meeting feeling energized and hopeful. But it wasn't just about the practical advice. It was the feeling that these people believed in her, maybe even more than she believed in herself.

Over the next few months, Lisa started implementing the group's suggestions. She reached out to that marketing agency contact And created not just one but three case studies. She even found a web developer to partner with on a big project.

But the biggest change was in Lisa herself. With each small success, her confidence grew. She started seeing herself not just as a freelancer but as a business owner. When a big opportunity came up, a chance to rebrand a well-known local company, Lisa didn't hesitate. She went for it. . . and she got it.

A year after joining the mastermind group, Lisa had doubled her income and was well on her way to starting her own small agency. More importantly, she had a support system she could rely on, people who celebrated her wins and helped her through tough times.

Your Turn: Building Your Tribe

So, how can you create your own network of allies and guides? Here are some steps to get you started:

1. Make a list of potential mentors, allies, and peers. Cast a wide net.

2. Reach out to one person on your list this week. Remember, start small.

3. Look for existing groups you could join. Professional associations, online communities, or local meetups can be great places to start.

4. If you can't find a group that fits, consider starting your own. Invite a few people you admire to join you for regular meetups or video calls.

5. Be a good tribe member. Offer support, celebrate others' successes, and be willing to be vulnerable about your own challenges.

Remember, building your tribe takes time. It's not about collecting a bunch of names in your contacts list. It's about creating real, meaningful relationships with people who support and challenge you.

Your tribe is out there. They're waiting to meet you, to support you, to help you become the best version of yourself. All you have to do is take that first step.

So, who will you reach out to first?

Your Secret Confidence Boosters

We've talked about building your tribe and creating your personal board of directors. Now, let's consider how to really make these relationships work for you. These are your secret weapons for boosting confidence and achieving your goals.

Regular Check-ins: Your Confidence Compass

Think of regular check-ins with your mentors or accountability partners as your confidence compass. They help you stay on track and navigate the sometimes choppy waters of personal and professional growth.

Here's how to make these check-ins work:

1. Set a schedule: Maybe it's monthly coffee with a mentor or weekly video calls with your accountability partner. The key is consistency.

2. Come prepared: Before each meeting, take some time to reflect. What progress have you made? What challenges are you facing? What specific advice do you need?

3. Set clear goals: Use these sessions to set concrete, achievable goals for the next period. Write them down. Share them with your mentor or partner.

4. Follow up: After each meeting, send a quick thank-you note summarizing what you discussed and your next steps. This shows respect for their time and helps you solidify your plans.

These check-ins aren't just about getting advice. They're about holding yourself accountable and celebrating your progress. Speaking of which...

Feedback: Your Growth Fuel

Feedback can be scary. But here's a secret: it's also one of the most powerful tools for building confidence. Why? Because it helps you improve. And when you improve, you feel more confident.

Here's how to make feedback work for you:

- Ask for it regularly: Don't wait for your annual review. Seek feedback often.

- Be specific: Instead of asking, "How am I doing?" try, "What's one thing I could improve in my presentations?"

- Listen without defensiveness: It's natural to want to explain or defend yourself. Resist that urge. Just listen and take notes.

- Say, thank you: Even if the feedback is tough to hear, express gratitude. It takes courage to give honest feedback.

- Act on it: Feedback is useless if you don't do anything with it. Make a plan to implement the suggestions you receive.

Remember, feedback isn't about tearing you down. It's about helping you grow. And growth is the foundation of true confidence.

Celebration: Your Confidence Fuel

When was the last time you really celebrated a win? Not just a quick "good job" to yourself, but a real celebration with your support network?

Celebrating your successes, big and small, is crucial for building and maintaining confidence. Here's why:

- It reinforces positive behavior

- It motivates you to keep going

- It helps you recognize your progress

- It strengthens your relationships with your support network

So, how do you celebrate effectively?

1. Acknowledge all wins: Did you finally make that scary phone call? Celebrate it. Landed a big client? Celebrate that, too. No win is too small.

2. Share with your tribe: Let your mentors, peers, and supporters know about your successes. They want to cheer you on!

3. Create rituals: Maybe it's a special dinner for big wins or a Friday dance party for weekly accomplishments. Having rituals makes celebration a habit.

4. Reflect on the journey: Don't just focus on the outcome. Celebrate the hard work, the lessons learned, and the growth along the way.

Luke's Transformation: From Self-Doubt to Leadership

Let's see how all this comes together in practice with Luke's story.

Luke was a talented software developer, but he struggled with self-doubt. He had ideas for improving his company's products, but he rarely spoke up in meetings. The thought of taking on leadership roles made him break out in a cold sweat.

That all changed when Luke decided to create his personal board of directors. He chose:

- His former college professor, known for her innovative thinking

- A senior developer at another company who Luke admired

- His cousin, a successful entrepreneur

- A character from his favorite sci-fi novel, known for their courage

- His high school track coach, who always pushed Luke to exceed his own expectations

Luke started having monthly "meetings" with his imaginary board. He'd present his challenges and listen to the advice he imagined they'd give. His professor would encourage him to think outside the box. His cousin would remind him of the importance of taking risks.

But Luke didn't stop there. He also reached out to a real-life mentor, a senior developer at his company. They started having bi-weekly check-ins. Luke would share his progress and get feedback on his ideas.

At first, the feedback was hard to hear. His mentor pointed out areas where Luke's technical skills needed improvement. But instead of getting discouraged, Luke used this as fuel. He created a learning plan and started tackling his weak spots.

Luke also joined a peer support group for developers. They met monthly to discuss challenges and celebrate wins. When Luke finally gathered the courage to present one of his ideas in a company meeting, his group threw him a virtual celebration.

As Luke implemented these strategies, something amazing happened. His confidence grew. He started speaking up more in meetings. His ideas were well-received, and he was assigned to lead a small project team.

There were still moments of self-doubt, of course. But now, Luke had the tools to manage them. When imposter syndrome struck, he'd imagine what his track coach would say: "You've put in the work, Luke. You've earned this."

A year later, Luke was promoted to team lead. During his acceptance speech, he thanked his mentor, his peer group, and his "personal board of directors." His colleagues looked confused at that last part, but Luke just smiled. He knew the power of his secret confidence boosters.

Your Turn: Activating Your Confidence Boosters

Ready to put these ideas into action? Here are your next steps:

1. Schedule regular check-ins: Set up a monthly meeting with a mentor or accountability partner. Come prepared with goals and questions.

2. Seek feedback: This week, ask for specific feedback from someone you trust. Remember to listen without defensiveness.

3. Celebrate a win: Think of a recent accomplishment, no matter how small. Share it with your support network and plan a small celebration.

4. Activate your board: If you've created an imaginary board of directors, start "consulting" them regularly. What would they say about your current challenges?

5. Track your progress: Keep a confidence journal. Note your wins, the feedback you've received, and how you've grown.

Remember, building confidence is a journey, not a destination. These tools are here to support you along the way. Use them regularly, and watch your confidence soar.

As we wrap up this chapter, think about how far you've come. You've identified toxic relationships, created your personal board of directors, and learned how to leverage your support network. You're well on your way to becoming the confident, successful person you're meant to be.

Chapter Ten

The 'What If' Game: Harnessing Your Imagination for Good

Reframe Worry into Possibility Powerhouses

W e've all been there. Lying awake at night, our minds racing with endless "what if" scenarios. What if I mess up that presentation? What if I can't pay my bills this month? What if I'm not good enough?

These nagging thoughts can be exhausting and paralyzing. But what if I told you that these same "what ifs" could be your secret weapon for success?

Welcome to the 'What If' Game, where we turn those pesky worries into powerful possibilities. It's time to flip the script and use your imagination for good.

Identifying Common Anxiety-Inducing "What If" Scenarios

First, let's look at some common worry-inducing thoughts:

- What if I fail?

- What if people laugh at me?

- What if I'm not smart enough?

- What if I can't handle the pressure?

- What if I make the wrong decision?

Sound familiar? These thoughts are like uninvited guests at a party - they show up unannounced and overstay their welcome. But instead of trying to kick them out, we're going to give them a makeover.

Flipping the Script: Turning Negatives into Positives

Here's where the magic happens. We're going to take those worries and flip them on their head. It's like turning a frown upside down but for your thoughts.

Let's start with "What if I fail?" This is a classic worry that holds many people back. But what if we looked at it differently? What if we asked instead, "What if I succeed beyond my wildest dreams?"

Suddenly, the energy shifts. Instead of feeling fear and doubt, you might feel excitement and anticipation. Your mind starts to explore possibilities rather than limitations.

Let's try another one. "What if people laugh at me?" becomes "What if my courage inspires people?" See how that changes things?

Here are a few more examples:

- "What if I'm not smart enough?" becomes "What if I'm capable of learning and growing more than I ever imagined?"

- "What if I can't handle the pressure?" turns into "What if I discover I'm stronger and more resilient than I thought?"

- "What if I make the wrong decision?" transforms to "What if every decision leads to valuable learning experiences?"

Building Confidence and Motivation

Now that we've flipped these scenarios, it's time to use them as fuel for your journey. These new "what ifs" aren't just positive thoughts; they're possibility powerhouses.

When you ask, "What if I succeed beyond my wildest dreams?" your brain starts to imagine what that success might look like. You might picture yourself confidently delivering that presentation, receiving applause, and maybe even a promotion. This mental imagery can boost your confidence and motivation.

These new scenarios act like a roadmap for your brain. They give you something positive to move towards rather than something negative to run away from. It's the difference between being chased by a bear and running towards an ice cream truck. Both might get you moving, but one is a lot more enjoyable!

Kathy's Transformation

Let's look at how this worked for Kathy, a graphic designer who dreamed of starting her own business.

Kathy had always wanted to start her own design agency, but every time she thought about it, her mind was flooded with worries. "What if I fail? What if I can't find clients? What if I'm not good enough?"

These thoughts kept Kathy stuck in her unfulfilling job for years. Then she learned about the 'What If' Game.

Kathy started to flip her worries:

- "What if I fail?" became "What if I create a thriving business that allows me to do work I love?"

- "What if I can't find clients?" turned into "What if I attract amazing clients who value my work?"

- "What if I'm not good enough?" transformed to "What if my unique style is exactly what some clients are looking for?"

As Kathy practiced this new way of thinking, she noticed a change. Instead of feeling paralyzed by fear, she felt excited about the possibilities. She started taking small steps towards her goal: creating a portfolio website, networking with other designers, and reaching out to potential clients.

Six months later, Kathy had enough clients to quit her job and focus on her business full-time. Two years after that, she was running a successful agency with a team of designers.

Kathy's success didn't come from ignoring her fears. It came from reframing them into possibilities and using those possibilities as motivation to take action.

Putting It Into Practice

So how can you start playing the 'What If' Game in your own life? Here are some steps to get you started:

1. Identify your worry-inducing "what ifs"

2. For each worry, ask yourself: "What's the opposite of this?"

3. Reframe your worry into a positive possibility

4. Visualize this new possibility in detail

5. Use this new scenario as motivation to take a small step forward

The goal isn't to eliminate all negative thoughts. It's to balance them with positive possibilities. It's about expanding your vision of what's possible.

The next time you find yourself spiraling into worry, pause and play the 'What If' Game. You might be surprised at the doors it opens in your mind and your life.

After all, what if this simple game changes everything for you? What if it's the key to unlocking your full potential? What if your greatest adventures and achievements are just waiting on the other side of a reframed "what if"?

There's only one way to find out. Are you ready to play?

Visualize Like a Champion Athlete

Ever wonder how Olympic athletes can perform at their peak under intense pressure? Sure, they train hard physically, but there's a secret weapon they use that you can't see: visualization.

Top performers across all fields, from sports to business, use this powerful mental technique to boost their performance. And guess what? You can, too.

Let's see how you can adopt these mental practices to enhance your own performance, no matter what field you're in.

Creating a Clear Mental Image of Your Desired Outcome

Visualization isn't just daydreaming. It's like watching a movie in your mind, but you're the director, star, and audience all rolled into one.

Start by getting clear on what you want to achieve. Maybe it's nailing a presentation at work, running your first 5K, or having a difficult conversation with a friend. Whatever it is, picture it in vivid detail.

Imagine yourself in that moment:

- What do you look like?

- How are you standing or moving?

- What's the expression on your face?

The clearer the image, the more powerful the effect. It's like giving your brain a detailed blueprint to follow.

Incorporating All Senses into Your Visualization

Here's where most people stop, but champion visualizers take it further. They don't just see their success - they feel it, hear it, even smell it.

Let's say you're visualizing giving a great presentation:

- See yourself standing confidently at the front of the room

- Hear the sound of your voice, strong and clear

- Feel the weight of the clicker in your hand

- Smell the coffee in the conference room

- Taste the mint you popped in your mouth for fresh breath

By engaging all your senses, you make the visualization more real to your brain. It's like a full dress rehearsal, but it's all happening in your mind.

Practicing Visualization Regularly

Like any skill, visualization gets better with practice. Most top performers do it daily, often right before they wake up or just before they fall asleep. These are times when your mind is naturally more relaxed and receptive.

But you don't need to spend hours on it. Even 5-10 minutes a day can make a big difference.

Try this: Set a reminder on your phone for a short visualization session each day. Start with just 2 minutes and work your way up.

And here's a pro tip: Visualize success, especially before important events. It's like giving your brain a pep talk and a game plan all at once.

Narrative: Michael Phelps' Pre-Race Visualization Routine

Let's look at how one of the greatest athletes of all time uses visualization: Michael Phelps, the most decorated Olympian in history.

Phelps didn't just visualize; he turned it into an art form. His coach, Bob Bowman, had him do a specific visualization routine twice a day, every day, from age 12 all the way through his Olympic career.

Here's what Phelps' routine looked like:

Every night before bed and every morning when he woke up, Phelps would close his eyes and play a "mental videotape" of his ideal race.

He'd imagine every detail:

- The feel of the water on his skin

- The sound of the crowd

- The smell of the chlorine

- The taste of victory

He visualized every stroke, every turn, even how he'd celebrate after winning. He'd imagine both the perfect race and races where things went wrong, mentally rehearsing how he'd handle any situation.

This routine became so ingrained that Phelps could calm himself before a race by playing his "videotape". It was like he'd already swum the race hundreds of times before he even dove into the pool.

The result? 28 Olympic medals, including 23 gold medals. Not too shabby!

Now, you might be thinking, "That's great for Michael Phelps, but I'm not an Olympic athlete." And you're right - you're not. But your brain doesn't know that.

When you visualize, your brain activates many of the same neural pathways as when you're actually doing the task. It's like a mental rehearsal that primes your brain and body for success.

Putting It Into Practice

So, how can you start visualizing like a champion? Here's a simple routine to get you started:

1. Choose Your Goal: Pick something specific you want to achieve.

2. Find a Quiet Spot: You need a place where you won't be disturbed.

3. Relax: Take a few deep breaths to calm your mind.

4. Create Your Mental Movie: Imagine achieving your goal in vivid detail. Use all your senses.

5. Feel the Emotion: Don't just see success; feel it. Let yourself experience the joy, pride, or excitement.

6. Practice Regularly: Do this for a few minutes each day, especially before big events.

Visualization isn't magic. It won't make you an Olympic athlete overnight. But when combined with actual practice and hard work, it can give you a significant edge.

Think of it as mental training. Just like you might go to the gym to build physical strength, visualization builds mental strength.

And here's the cool part: The more you practice visualization, the better you'll get at it. Over time, your mental images will become clearer, more detailed, and more powerful.

You might start noticing changes in your performance. Maybe you feel calmer under pressure. Maybe you bounce back faster from setbacks. Or maybe you just feel more confident going into challenging situations.

These are all signs that your visualization practice is working.

So why not give it a try? Pick a goal you're working towards right now. Close your eyes and spend a few minutes visualizing your success. See it, hear it, feel it.

You've got nothing to lose and potentially a lot to gain. After all, if it's good enough for Olympic champions, it might just be good enough for you, too.

Remember, your mind is a powerful tool. By learning to visualize like a champion athlete, you're not just dreaming of success; you're mentally rehearsing it. And that mental rehearsal can be the difference between "I wish I could" and "I knew I could".

So go ahead, close your eyes, and start your mental movie. Your starring role in your own success story is waiting.

Visualizing Your Future Self in Action

Have you ever wondered what your life could look like if everything went right? Not just okay, not just good, but absolutely amazing? That's what we're going to explore in this section. We're going to create a vivid, detailed vision of your best possible future self.

This isn't just a fun daydreaming exercise (though it is fun!) It's a powerful tool that can guide your actions, motivate you, and help you make better decisions. It's like creating a roadmap for your life, with your ideal self as the destination.

Defining Your Ideal Self

Let's start by defining your ideal self in various aspects of life. We're going to focus on three key areas: career, relationships, and health.

Grab a pen and paper, or open a new document on your computer. We're going to do some brainstorming.

Career:

- What kind of work are you doing?

- How do you feel about your job?

- What have you achieved?

- How much are you earning?

- What impact are you making?

Don't hold back here. If you've always dreamed of being a best-selling author, write it down. If you want to start your own company, put it on paper. This is your ideal future, so make it as awesome as you want.

Relationships:

- Who are the important people in your life?

- What kind of partner are you (if you want a partner)?

- How do you treat your friends and family?

- What kind of friend/partner/family member are you?

- How do others see you?

Health:

- How do you feel physically?

- What does your body look like?

- What kind of energy do you have?

- What are your eating habits?

- How often do you exercise?

We're imagining your ideal self here. If you want to run marathons, write it down. If you want to feel strong and flexible, note it.

Imagining a Day in the Life

Now that we have some broad strokes let's zoom in and imagine a typical day in the life of your future self. This is where things get really fun and detailed.

Start from the moment you wake up:

- What time is it?

- Where are you?

- Who's with you?

Take us through your morning routine:

- What do you eat for breakfast?

- How do you get ready for the day?

- What are you wearing?

Now, imagine your work day:

- Where do you go?

- What tasks do you tackle?

- Who do you interact with?

- How do you feel about your work?

Don't forget about your evening:

- What do you do after work?

- Who do you spend time with?

- How do you relax?

- What do you eat for dinner?

Finally, think about how you end your day:

- What's your bedtime routine?

- How do you feel as you're falling asleep?

As you're doing this, try to engage all your senses. What do you see, hear, smell, taste, and feel throughout this ideal day?

The more detail you can add, the more real this future will feel to you. And the more real it feels the more power it has to guide and motivate you.

Using Your Vision as a Tool

Now that you have this vivid vision of your ideal future self, how do you use it?

First, it's a powerful source of motivation. When you're feeling stuck or discouraged, revisit this vision. Remind yourself of what you're working towards. It's like having a personal cheerleader in your mind, always ready to boost your spirits.

Second, it can be used as a decision-making tool. When you're faced with a choice, ask yourself: "Which option brings me closer to my ideal future?" This can help you make decisions that align with your long-term goals, even when the short-term path might be tougher.

Lastly, use it to guide your daily actions. Look at your current habits and routines. How can you adjust them to be more in line with your future self? Maybe your ideal self meditates every morning. You could start with just a minute of meditation each day, gradually working up to more.

Remember, the goal isn't to magically transform into this ideal self overnight. It's to use this vision as a compass, guiding you in the right direction one step at a time.

The Jim Carrey $10 Million Check Visualization

Let's look at a famous example of the power of visualization: Jim Carrey's $10 million check.

Back in 1985, Jim Carrey was a struggling comedian. He was broke, unknown, and things weren't looking great. But he had a dream and a powerful belief in visualization.

One night, he drove his beat-up Toyota to the Hollywood Hills. Looking out over Los Angeles, he wrote himself a check for $10 million "for acting services rendered." He dated it Thanksgiving 1995, giving himself 10 years to make it happen.

He carried that check in his wallet for years, looking at it every day, visualizing what it would be like to actually earn that much money as an actor.

Fast forward to 1994. Carrey landed a role in the movie Dumb and Dumber. His pay for that movie? $10 million.

Now, did visualization alone make Jim Carrey a success? Of course not. He worked incredibly hard, honing his craft and taking every opportunity he could. But that vivid vision of success, that concrete goal he could see and touch every day, kept him motivated through the tough times.

It's Your Turn to Visualize

You might be thinking, "That's great for Jim Carrey, but I'm not trying to be a movie star." And you're right. Your vision doesn't have to be about fame or fortune. It's about what success and fulfillment mean to you.

Maybe your version of a $10 million check is a picture of the house you want to own, a mock-up of the book you want to write, or a photo of the place you want to travel.

Whatever it is, make it concrete. Write it down, draw it, and create a vision board. Make it something you can see and touch every day.

Then, like Jim Carrey, carry it with you. Look at it often. Let it remind you of what you're working towards.

But here's the key: don't just visualize and wait for magic to happen. Use your vision as fuel for action. Let it guide your choices, motivate your efforts, and inspire you to keep pushing forward, even when things get tough.

Remember, your future self is counting on you. Every small step you take today is creating the person you'll become tomorrow. So dream big, visualize vividly, and then take action to make it happen.

Your best possible future is waiting. Are you ready to start creating it?

Unleash "What If" to Conquer Challenges

We've all faced problems that seemed impossible to solve. You know, those sticky situations where you feel stuck, out of ideas, and ready to throw in the towel. But what if I told you that the key to unlocking these challenges is right there in your imagination?

Let's show how we can use "What if?" thinking to generate creative solutions to even the toughest problems.

Brainstorming Multiple "What If?" Scenarios

The first step in this process is to let your imagination run wild. When faced with a problem, start by asking yourself, "What if. . .?" and then let your mind explore all sorts of possibilities, no matter how crazy they might seem at first.

Let's say you're trying to increase sales for your small business. Your "What if?" questions might look like this:

- What if we offered a buy-one-get-one-free deal?

- What if we partnered with a complementary business?

- What if we created a viral social media challenge?

- What if we gave away free samples in busy areas?

- What if we offered a money-back guarantee?

The key here is quantity over quality. Don't judge your ideas yet. Just let them flow. The crazier, the better!

Evaluating Scenarios for Feasibility and Impact

Once you've got a good list of "What if?" scenarios, it's time to put on your practical hat. Look at each idea and ask yourself two questions:

1. How feasible is this?

2. What impact could this have?

Rate each idea on a scale of 1-10 for both feasibility and potential impact. This will help you identify the ideas that are both doable and potentially game-changing.

For our small business example, it might look like this:

- Buy-one-get-one deal: Feasibility 8, Impact 6

- Business partnership: Feasibility 5, Impact 9

- Viral social media challenge: Feasibility 3, Impact 10

- Free samples: Feasibility 7, Impact 7

- Money-back guarantee: Feasibility 9, Impact 8

Choosing and Developing Promising Ideas

Now that you've evaluated your ideas focus on the ones with the highest combined scores for feasibility and impact. These are your golden tickets - the ideas most worth pursuing.

For each of these top ideas, develop a simple action plan:

1. What specific steps would you need to take to implement this idea?

2. What resources would you need?

3. What potential obstacles might you face, and how could you overcome them?

4. What timeline would be realistic for implementation?

This process turns your "What if?" scenarios from vague ideas into concrete plans of action.

The Birth of the Post-it Note

Let's look at a real-world example of how "What if?" thinking led to a revolutionary invention: the Post-it note.

In 1968, Dr. Spencer Silver, a scientist at 3M, was trying to develop a super-strong adhesive. Instead, he accidentally created a weak adhesive that could be peeled off surfaces without leaving a mark. At first, this seemed like a failure. After all, who wants a weak glue?

But Silver didn't give up. He kept asking, "What if?" What if this weak adhesive could be useful for something?

For years, Silver promoted his "solution without a problem" within 3M, but without success. Then, in 1974, his colleague Art Fry had a "What if?" moment of his own.

Fry sang in his church choir and was frustrated that the bookmarks in his hymnal kept falling out. He thought, "What if we put Silver's adhesive on paper to create repositionable bookmarks?"

This "What if?" led to experiments, which led to prototypes, which eventually led to the Post-it note - a product that has generated billions in sales for 3M.

The key lessons from this story:

1. Sometimes, "failures" can lead to unexpected successes if you keep an open mind.

2. Persistence pays off. Silver didn't give up on his idea for years.

3. Collaboration can spark new "What if?" ideas, it took both Silver and Fry to create the Post-it.

4. "What if?" thinking can turn everyday annoyances (like falling bookmarks) into innovative solutions.

Recap of Key Points

Let's review what we've covered in this chapter:

1. We learned how to transform negative "what ifs" into positive scenarios, turning worry into possibility.

2. We explored visualization techniques used by top athletes to enhance performance, showing how mental rehearsal can prepare us for real-world challenges.

3. We created a detailed vision of our ideal future selves, providing a roadmap for personal growth and decision-making.

4. Finally, we applied "What if?" thinking to problem-solving, using imaginative brainstorming to generate creative solutions.

These techniques all harness the power of your imagination to drive personal growth and overcome challenges.

Action Steps

Ready to put these ideas into practice? Here are some concrete steps you can take:

1. Identify three negative "what ifs" in your life and reframe them positively. For example, "What if I fail?" becomes "What if I succeed beyond my wildest dreams?"

2. Practice visualizing success for an upcoming important event. Spend 5-10 minutes each day this week imagining the event going perfectly, engaging all your senses in the visualization.

3. Write a detailed description of your ideal day five years from now. Include specifics about your career, relationships, health, and daily routine.

4. Use the "What if?" technique to brainstorm solutions for a current challenge you're facing. Generate at least 10 "What if?" scenarios, then evaluate them for feasibility and potential impact.

These techniques get more powerful with practice. The more you use them, the more natural and effective they'll become.

As we've seen, harnessing your imagination can be a powerful tool for personal growth and problem-solving. We've explored how to reframe negative thoughts, visualize success, create a vision for your future, and use "What if?" thinking to generate creative solutions.

But imagination alone isn't enough. To truly transform your life, you need to turn these mental strategies into concrete action. In the next chapter, we'll explore how to do just that. We'll dive into the art of turning small steps into quantum leaps, creating a practical roadmap to achieve the goals you've visualized.

Get ready to move from imagination to action, from "What if?" to "Let's do this!" Your journey of transformation is just beginning.

Chapter Eleven

Action Alchemy: Turning Small Steps into Quantum Leaps

Small Steps, Massive Impact

You've probably heard the saying, "A journey of a thousand miles begins with a single step." It's a nice thought, but let's be real; who has time for a thousand-mile journey these days? We're all busy juggling work and family and trying to remember if we fed the cat this morning. But here's the thing: that ancient proverb is onto something big.

Let's talk about small steps and how they can lead to massive changes in your life. It's like magic but without the top hat and rabbit.

Daily habits shape long-term outcomes

Think about your daily routine. Maybe you hit the snooze button three times, grab a coffee, and rush out the door. Or perhaps you're the type who wakes up at 5 AM for a morning jog (if so, we're both impressed and slightly suspicious). Whatever your routine, it's made up of small actions you repeat day after day.

These little actions might seem insignificant, but they're secretly running the show. They're like tiny directors in the movie of your life, quietly influencing every scene.

- Your morning coffee ritual? It's setting the tone for your entire day.

- That quick scroll through social media before bed? It's affecting your sleep quality.

- The way you greet your coworkers? It's shaping your professional relationships.

Over time, these small actions add up. They become the building blocks of your life, determining your health, relationships, career success, and overall happiness.

The power of incremental progress

Now, let's talk about the magic of small improvements. Imagine you could get just 1% better at something every day. Sounds pretty doable, right? You'd improve so much from the day you started.

This is the power of incremental progress. It's like compound interest for your life. Small, consistent improvements snowball over time, creating massive changes.

But here's the catch: it works both ways. If you get 1% worse each day, you'll decline pretty quickly. So, the question is: which direction are your daily habits taking you?

Overcoming inertia through tiny steps

Let's face it: starting something new is hard. Whether it's a diet, a workout routine, or learning a new skill, that first step can feel like trying to push a boulder uphill; this is where tiny steps come in handy.

Instead of trying to overhaul your entire life overnight, focus on actions so small they seem almost laughable. Want to start exercising? Don't aim for an hour at the gym; start with a single push-up. Want to eat healthier? Don't revamp your whole diet - just add one extra vegetable to your plate.

These tiny actions serve two purposes:

1. They're so easy that you have no excuse not to do them.

2. They help you build momentum and overcome inertia.

Once you start moving, it becomes easier to keep going. It's like giving that boulder a tiny nudge; once it starts rolling, it picks up speed on its own.

Steph's journey from couch potato to marathon runner through 5-minute daily walks

Let's look at how this works in real life. Meet Steph, a self-proclaimed couch potato who transformed her life through tiny steps.

Steph had always dreamed of running a marathon, but the thought of training was overwhelming. She'd tried to start running programs before but always gave up after a few days, feeling discouraged and out of breath.

One day, Steph decided to try a different approach. Instead of forcing herself to run, she committed to taking a 5-minute walk every day. Just 5 minutes, no more, no less.

At first, it felt almost silly. What difference could a 5-minute walk make? But Steph stuck with it. Some days, she'd walk around her living room. On other days, she'd stroll down the street. The important thing was that she did it every single day.

After a few weeks, something interesting happened. Steph found herself looking forward to her daily walks. Sometimes, she'd even walk for 10 or 15 minutes without realizing it.

As the weeks turned into months, Steph's 5-minute walks gradually evolved. She started walking faster, then alternating between walking and jogging. Before she knew it, she was running for 30 minutes straight.

Two years after starting her 5-minute daily walks, Steph crossed the finish line of her first marathon. She wasn't the fastest runner, but she finished, something she never thought possible when she was stuck on the couch.

Steph's story shows the power of small steps. She didn't try to become a marathon runner overnight. Instead, she focused on a tiny, manageable action and let it snowball over time.

The takeaway? Don't underestimate the power of small actions. They might seem insignificant in the moment, but they have the potential to create massive change over time.

So, what tiny step could you take today? Maybe it's drinking an extra glass of water, spending five minutes tidying up, or sending a quick message to a friend you've been meaning to catch up with.

You don't need to overhaul your entire life overnight. Start small, be consistent, and watch as those tiny steps lead you to big places. Who knows? Your 5-minute walk today could be the first step towards your own marathon, whatever that looks like for you.

And hey, even if you don't end up running a marathon, at least you'll have gotten off the couch. That's a win in our book.

Pinpoint Your Productivity Powerhouses

Let's talk about getting stuff done without losing your mind. You know those days when you're running around like a headless chicken, but at the end of it all, you feel like you've achieved. . . we've all been there. But what if I told you there's a way to do less and achieve more? Sounds like a late-night infomercial, right? But stick with me because this is where things get interesting.

Welcome to the world of Productivity Powerhouses. It's not about working harder or longer. It's about working smarter. It's like finding the cheat codes for your life.

The Pareto Principle (80/20 rule) in personal development

First up, let's talk about this fancy-sounding thing called the Pareto Principle. Don't worry; it's not as complicated as it sounds. In fact, you've probably seen it in action without even realizing it.

The Pareto Principle, also known as the 80/20 rule, suggests that roughly 80% of your results come from 20% of your efforts. It's like that one pair of comfy jeans you wear 80% of the time, even though your closet is bursting with options.

In personal development, this principle is a game-changer. It means that a small number of your actions are responsible for most of your progress. The trick is figuring out which actions those are.

- Maybe 20% of your workout routine is giving you 80% of your fitness gains.

- Perhaps 20% of your study time is yielding 80% of your learning.

- It could be that 20% of your daily tasks are producing 80% of your productivity.

The key is to identify these high-impact activities and focus on them. It's like finding the magic lever that makes everything else easier.

Aligning actions with core values and goals

Now, let's get a bit personal. What really matters to you? What are your big dreams, your core values? These aren't just fluffy questions; they're the compass that should guide your actions.

When your actions align with your values and goals, magic happens. You're not just busy; you're productive in a way that feels meaningful and satisfying. It's the difference between spinning your wheels and actually getting somewhere.

Take a moment to think about your top three values or goals. Maybe it's family, career growth, and health. Now, look at how you spend your time. Do your actions reflect these priorities? If not, it's time for a change.

Eliminating low-value activities to free up time and energy

Here's where things get a bit ruthless, but in a good way. It's time to Marie Kondo your to-do list. Look at everything you do in a day and ask yourself: "Does this spark joy. . .or results?"

Low-value activities are the sneaky time-thieves that leave you feeling busy but unfulfilled. They're the endless social media scrolling, the meetings that could have been emails, and the perfectionist tendencies that keep you polishing a task long after it's good enough.

Cutting these out can feel scary at first. You might worry about missing out or letting people down. But here's the thing: by eliminating these low-value activities, you're making room for the stuff that really matters.

- Try tracking your time for a week. You might be surprised where it's actually going.

- Look for tasks you can delegate, automate, or simply eliminate.

- Learn to say no to commitments that don't align with your priorities.

Every "no" to something unimportant is a "yes" to something that matters.

Now, let's see how this all works in the real world. Meet Tom, a CEO who transformed his company by focusing on what really mattered.

Narrative: CEO Tom's transformation of his company by focusing on three key metrics

Tom was the CEO of a mid-sized tech company. His team were burnt out, and despite all their efforts, profits were flatlining.

One day, while doom-scrolling through business articles (we've all been there), Tom stumbled upon the concept of the Pareto Principle. Intrigued, he decided to apply it to his business.

Tom gathered his team and asked a simple question: "What are the few things that really move the needle for our company?" After hours of heated debate (and several pizzas), they identified three key metrics:

1. Customer satisfaction scores

2. New feature adoption rates

3. Employee productivity

These became their North Star. Instead of trying to improve everything at once, they laser-focused on these three areas.

The changes were small at first. They started sending out quick, two-question surveys to customers after each interaction. They created a "Feature of the Week" campaign to highlight new tools. They introduced "Focus Fridays," where employees could work on projects without interruptions.

Tom made some tough calls to make room for these initiatives. He cut several ongoing projects that weren't directly tied to their key metrics. He reduced the number of meetings by half. He even decided to pause their annual company picnic (though he promised to bring it back bigger and better once they'd turned things around).

At first, there was pushback. People worried about the projects being cut and the changes to their routines. But Tom stood firm, reminding everyone of their three key focus areas.

Slowly but surely, things started to change. Customer satisfaction scores began to climb. More users were adopting new features. And despite working fewer hours, employees were getting more done.

Six months later, the company saw its first significant profit increase in years. By the one-year mark, they had doubled their growth rate. And Tom? He was down to a 50-hour work week and actually taking weekends off.

The lesson? By focusing on a few key areas and ruthlessly eliminating everything else, Tom and his team achieved more than they ever had before.

So, what's the takeaway from all this? It's simple: not all actions are created equal. Some pack a much bigger punch than others. Your job is to find those high-impact activities and focus on them like a laser.

Start by identifying your own "key metrics" - the few areas that will make the biggest difference in your life. Then, be ruthless about aligning your time and energy with these priorities. Cut out the fluff, the busywork, the "should-dos" that don't really matter.

It might feel uncomfortable at first. You might worry that you're not doing enough. But remember Tom's story. Less can indeed be more if you're doing the right less.

So, what are your productivity powerhouses? What are the few actions that will give you the biggest bang for your buck? Find them, focus on them, and watch as your life transforms - one high-impact action at a time.

And hey, if all else fails, at least you'll have more time for Netflix. But something tells me you're ready for bigger things.

Effortless Roadmap to Personal Success

Let's talk about success. Not the kind you see in glossy magazines or on social media, but real, personal success. The kind that makes you feel like you're winning at life, even if you're still wearing yesterday's pajamas.

Welcome to your Effortless Roadmap to Personal Success. Now, I know what you're thinking. "Effortless? Yeah, right. And pigs might fly." But stick with me here. We're not talking about success without effort. We're talking about success that feels natural like you're flowing downstream instead of constantly swimming against the current.

Leveraging personal strengths and preferences

First things first, let's talk about you. Yes, you. What makes you tick? What lights you up? What are you naturally good at?

Too often, we try to force ourselves into someone else's mold of success. It's like trying to fit a square peg into a round hole. Sure, if you hammer hard enough, you might make it work. But it's going to be a struggle, and frankly, it's going to hurt.

Instead, let's play to your strengths. Are you a night owl? Stop trying to force yourself into that 5 AM club. Are you great at coming up with ideas but struggle with follow-through? Partner with someone who loves ticking off to-do lists.

- Think about times when you've been in 'the zone'; what were you doing?

- Consider compliments you often receive; they might point to hidden strengths.

- Reflect on tasks you enjoy so much you lose track of time.

These are clues to your natural strengths and preferences. They're like your personal superpowers. Use them!

Breaking down big goals into manageable tasks

Now, let's talk about those big, juicy goals you have. The ones that make your heart race with excitement. . . and maybe a little fear. They're great, but they can also be overwhelming. It's like standing at the bottom of Mount Everest in flip-flops.

The secret? Break it down. And then break it down again. And again. Until you have steps so small, they're almost laughable.

Want to write a book? Start with writing one sentence a day. Want to run a marathon? Begin with a 5-minute walk. Want to start a business? Focus on making your first dollar.

These tiny steps serve two purposes:

1. They make starting feel less daunting.

2. They give you a clear path forward.

It's like having a GPS for your goals. Instead of staring at your destination in the distance, you can focus on the next turn, the next step.

Building momentum through early wins

Here's where the magic happens. Those tiny steps we talked about? They're not just about making progress. They're about building momentum.

Every small win gives you a little burst of motivation. It's like a snowball rolling down a hill, gathering more snow and speed as it goes. Before you know it, you've got an unstoppable force of achievement.

The key is to celebrate these early wins. Did you write that one sentence? Awesome! Give yourself a high five. Did you take that 5-minute walk? You're a rock star!

These celebrations might feel silly at first. But they're actually rewiring your brain, associating progress with positive feelings. And that's what will keep you going when things get tough.

Now, let's see how this works in real life. Meet Emily, an aspiring novelist who turned 15 minutes a day into a finished book.

Anecdote: Emily's success in writing a novel by committing to just 15 minutes of daily writing

Emily had always dreamed of writing a novel. She had notebooks full of ideas, characters sketched out in her mind, and a story burning to be told. But every time she sat down to write, she froze. The task seemed too big, too daunting.

One day, Emily decided to try a different approach. Instead of trying to write her magnum opus in one go, she committed to writing for just 15 minutes a day. No more, no less.

At first, it felt almost pointless. What could she possibly accomplish in 15 minutes? But Emily stuck with it. Some days, she'd write a few sentences. On other days, she'd flesh out a character description or brainstorm plot points.

As the days turned into weeks, something interesting happened. Emily found herself looking forward to her daily writing sessions. Sometimes, she'd even write for longer than 15 minutes, caught up in the flow of her story.

Emily celebrated every small win. Wrote for 15 minutes? That's a win. Came up with a clever plot twist? Definite win. Figured out her main character's favorite ice cream flavor? You bet that's a win.

These little victories kept Emily going, even on days when the words didn't flow easily. She knew that showing up was half the battle.

Six months into her 15-minute-a-day habit, Emily had a rough first draft of her novel. It wasn't perfect, but it was there, 60,000 words that didn't exist before.

Emily was amazed. She'd written a novel, all in 15-minute increments. More importantly, she'd proven to herself that she could do it. That snowball of early wins had turned into an avalanche of achievement.

So, what can we learn from Emily's story? It's simple: small, consistent actions that are aligned with your natural rhythms and celebrated along the way can lead to big results.

The takeaway? Your road to success doesn't have to be paved with sweat and tears. It can be a series of small, enjoyable steps that align with who you are and how you work best.

Start by identifying your strengths and preferences. Are you a morning person or a night owl? Do you work best in short bursts or long stretches? Do you thrive on variety or prefer routine? Use this self-knowledge to design your approach.

Next, take that big, scary goal and break it down into tiny, manageable pieces. Make them so small that you can't help but succeed. You're not aiming for perfection here. You're aiming for progress.

Finally, celebrate every win, no matter how small. Did you make your bed this morning? Boom! Celebrate. Did you drink a glass of water instead of soda? You're killing it! Celebrate.

These celebrations aren't just feel-good fluff. They're the fuel that will keep you going when motivation wanes. They're the breadcrumbs that will lead you back to your path when you get lost.

Your road to success is uniquely yours. It doesn't have to look like anyone else's. It doesn't have to be a grueling uphill battle. It can be a series of small, enjoyable steps that feel almost effortless.

So, what's your 15-minute daily habit going to be? What small step can you take today towards your big goal? Remember, it doesn't have to be perfect. It just has to be a start.

And hey, if you mess up today, there's always tomorrow. The road to success isn't a straight line. It's more like a squiggly doodle with lots of detours and pitstops. But as long as you keep moving forward, even in tiny 15-minute increments, you'll get there.

Your effortless roadmap to success is waiting. All you have to do is take that first small step. So, what are you waiting for? Your 15 minutes starts now.

Doubt-Busting Steps to Self-Confidence

Alright, let's talk about something we've all felt at some point: self-doubt. You know, that little voice in your head that whispers, "Are you sure you can do this?" It's like having a personal rain cloud following you around, raining on your parade every chance it gets.

But here's the thing: self-doubt isn't the boss of you. In fact, it's more like that annoying coworker who always has something negative to say. You can't fire them, but you can definitely learn to tune them out.

Welcome to your Doubt-Busting Steps to Self-Confidence. We're about to turn that rain cloud into your personal cheerleading squad. Sounds impossible? Stick with me, and you'll see how taking action can be your secret weapon against self-doubt.

The role of evidence in changing beliefs

Let's start with a simple truth: your brain believes what you show it. It's like a jury; it needs evidence to make a decision. And guess what? You're the one presenting the case.

Every time you take action, you're providing evidence. Evidence that you're capable, that you can follow through, that you can handle challenges. It's like building a case file against your self-doubt.

- Did you make that phone call you've been dreading? That's evidence.

- Did you try that new recipe? More evidence.

- Did you speak up in that meeting? Yep, you guessed it, evidence.

Each action, no matter how small, is a piece of evidence that contradicts your self-doubt. Over time, these pieces of evidence add up, and your brain has no choice but to revise its verdict.

Reframing failures as learning opportunities

Now, let's talk about the F-word. No, not that one; I'm talking about failure. It's a word that can send shivers down your spine. But what if I told you that failure isn't your enemy? In fact, it might just be your best teacher.

Every failure is a learning opportunity in disguise. It's like life is giving you a personalized lesson plan. Didn't get that job? Now you know how to improve your interview skills. Burnt that cake? Now you know to set a timer next time.

The key is to reframe these experiences. Instead of thinking, "I failed," try, "I learned." It's not just positive thinking; it's a more accurate way of looking at the situation.

- Ask yourself: "What can I learn from this?"

- Look for patterns in your failures; they might point to areas for improvement.

- Remember: every expert was once a beginner who kept going despite setbacks.

Celebrating small victories to boost motivation

Let's be real: big wins don't happen every day. But you know what can happen every day? Small victories. And these little wins are the secret sauce to boosting your motivation and silencing your inner critic.

Did you make your bed this morning? Victory! Did you drink water instead of soda? Another win! Did you resist the urge to check your phone for a whole hour? You're on fire!

These might seem trivial, but they're not. Each small victory is a vote of confidence in yourself. It's proof that you can set a goal and achieve it. And the more you prove this to yourself, the less power your self-doubt has.

So celebrate these wins. Do a little dance, give yourself a high five, or treat yourself to something special. The more you associate taking action with positive feelings, the more motivated you'll be to keep going.

Now, let's see how this works in real life. Meet Mark, who went from a shy introvert to a confident public speaker through gradual exposure.

Mark's journey from a shy introvert to a confident public speaker through gradual exposure

Mark was the kind of guy who'd rather eat a live spider than speak in public. The mere thought of standing in front of a crowd made his palms sweat and his heart race. But Mark had a dream: he wanted to share his ideas with the world.

Instead of diving headfirst into public speaking (which, let's be honest, would have been a disaster), Mark decided to take baby steps.

He started by recording himself speaking in his room. No audience, just him and his phone camera. At first, he could barely get through a sentence without stumbling. But he kept at it, recording a one-minute video every day.

After a month, Mark felt ready for the next step. He joined a small online group where members practiced public speaking. Mark learned something new each time.

As weeks turned into months, Mark gradually increased his exposure. He spoke at small gatherings of friends and then at local community meetings. Each time, he felt nervous, but he reframed it as excitement. Each speech, regardless of how it went, was evidence that he could do it.

Mark celebrated every small victory. Spoke for a full minute without saying "um"? Victory dance! Made eye contact with the audience? Time for a treat! These celebrations kept him going, even when his inner critic tried to discourage him.

A year after starting his journey, Mark was invited to speak at a local TEDx event. As he stood on that red circular carpet, facing an audience of hundreds, he felt something he'd never experienced before: confidence.

Mark's hands weren't shaking. His voice was steady. And as he delivered his talk, he realized something amazing: he was actually enjoying himself.

The shy introvert who once couldn't speak in front of a mirror had become a confident public speaker through small, consistent actions and a willingness to reframe his experiences.

So, what can we learn from Mark's story? It's simple: action is the antidote to self-doubt. Every step you take, no matter how small, is a blow against your inner critic.

Here's how you can apply this in your own life:

1. Start small. Really small. What's the tiniest step you can take towards your goal?

2. Collect evidence. Keep a record of your actions and achievements, no matter how small. This is your ammunition against self-doubt.

3. Reframe failures. When things don't go as planned, ask yourself, "What can I learn from this?" Turn every setback into a stepping stone.

4. Celebrate small victories. Did you take action today? That's worth celebrating! Create positive associations by taking steps towards your goals.

5. Gradually increase your challenges. As you build confidence, slowly stretch your comfort zone. It's about progress, not perfection.

Remember, confidence isn't something you're born with - it's something you build. And you build it through action, one small step at a time.

So, what small step will you take today? What tiny action can you commit to that will start building your case against self-doubt? It doesn't have to be big. It just has to be a start.

And hey, if you're feeling hesitant, that's okay. Doubt is normal. But don't let it stop you. As Mark showed us, even the most anxious introvert can become a confident speaker. All it takes is a willingness to start and the courage to keep going.

Your journey to confidence starts now. Take that first small step. Collect that first piece of evidence. Celebrate that first tiny victory. Before you know it, you'll be looking back, amazed at how far you've come.

And your inner critic? It'll still be there, but it'll be more like background noise - easy to ignore as you confidently stride towards your goals. So go ahead, take that step. Your confident future self is cheering you on.

Chapter Twelve

The Identity Shift: Becoming the Person You Want to Be

Identity's Hidden Influence on Personal Transformation

Have you ever wondered why some people seem to achieve their goals effortlessly while others struggle? The secret might be hiding in plain sight; it's all about identity.

Our identity, or how we see ourselves, has a powerful influence on our actions, habits, and, ultimately, our success. It's like an invisible force guiding our decisions and shaping our lives. But here's the kicker: most of us don't even realize it's happening.

Let's examine how identity plays a crucial role in personal transformation.

The Power of Self-Fulfilling Prophecies

You've probably heard the saying, "Whether you think you can or you think you can't, you're right." This isn't just a catchy phrase; it's backed by psychological research on self-fulfilling prophecies.

A self-fulfilling prophecy is a belief that leads to its own fulfillment. In other words, if you believe something about yourself, you're likely to act in ways that make it come true.

Here's how it works:

1. You have a belief about yourself.

2. This belief influences your actions.

3. Your actions create results that confirm your initial belief.

For example, if you believe you're bad at public speaking, you might avoid opportunities to speak in front of others. This lack of practice makes you less skilled, confirming your initial belief. It's a vicious cycle.

But here's the good news: this cycle can work in your favor, too. If you believe you're a confident public speaker, you're more likely to seek out speaking opportunities, practice more, and improve your skills.

The key is to be aware of your beliefs and consciously choose the ones that serve you.

Identity-Based Habits vs. Goal-Based Habits

When it comes to creating lasting change, identity-based habits are far more powerful than goal-based habits.

Goal-based habits focus on what you want to achieve. Identity-based habits focus on who you want to become.

Let's look at an example. Say you want to get in shape.

A goal-based approach might be: "I want to lose 20 pounds."

An identity-based approach would be: "I am a healthy person who takes care of my body."

The goal-based approach can work in the short term, but it often fails in the long run. Once you reach your goal (or if you fail to reach it), you might lose motivation.

The identity-based approach, on the other hand, creates lasting change. When you see yourself as a healthy person, making healthy choices becomes part of who you are, not just something you do.

The Impact of Identity on Decision-Making and Willpower

Your identity doesn't just influence your habits; it also affects your decision-making and willpower.

When faced with a choice, we often ask ourselves, "What would someone like me do in this situation?" Our actions align with our self-image.

If you see yourself as a disciplined person, you're more likely to make choices that require self-control. You're not relying on willpower alone; you're acting in alignment with your identity.

This is why identity shifts can be so powerful. When you change how you see yourself, you change the entire framework for your decisions.

Donna's Identity Shift

Let's look at how this plays out in real life with the story of Donna, a struggling entrepreneur.

Donna had been running her small marketing agency for five years. While she was getting by, she felt stuck. She worked long hours, took on any client she could get, and constantly worried about making ends meet.

Donna's identity was that of a "small business owner just trying to survive." This identity influenced her actions:

- She undercharged for her services

- She was afraid to turn down clients, even if they weren't a good fit

- She didn't invest in growing her skills or her team

Then, Donna had a revelation. She realized that her identity was holding her back. She decided to make a shift.

Instead of seeing herself as a "small business owner," Donna started to think of herself as an "industry leader." This simple shift changed everything.

With her new identity, Donna:

- Raised her prices to reflect the value she provided

- Became selective about the clients she worked with

- Invested in advanced training for herself and her team

- Started speaking at industry events and writing thought leadership articles

The results were dramatic. Within a year, Donna's revenue had doubled. She was working with dream clients and had built a team she was proud of. Most importantly, she felt confident and fulfilled in her work.

Donna's story shows the power of an identity shift. By changing how she saw herself, she changed her actions, which in turn changed her results.

Putting It Into Practice

So, how can you harness the power of identity for your own transformation? Here are some steps to get started:

1. Reflect on your current identity. How do you see yourself? What labels do you use?

2. Identify any limiting beliefs tied to your current identity.

3. Envision the person you want to become. What would this person believe about themselves?

4. Choose a new identity that aligns with your goals and values.

5. Start small. Look for tiny ways to act in alignment with your new identity every day.

6. Be patient. Identity shifts take time, but with consistent effort, they can lead to profound changes.

You have the power to choose who you want to be. Your identity isn't set in stone - it's a choice you make every day through your actions and beliefs.

By aligning your identity with your aspirations, you can unlock new levels of motivation, confidence, and success. It's not about becoming a different person - it's about becoming the best version of yourself.

Forge Your Inner Champion Mindset

Ever feel like there's a little voice in your head constantly telling you that you're not good enough? You're not alone. We all have an inner critic, but here's the thing: you have the power to turn that critic into your biggest cheerleader. Let's look at how you can forge an inner champion mindset.

Identifying and Challenging Limiting Beliefs

First things first, we need to shine a light on those pesky limiting beliefs. These are the thoughts that hold you back; the "I can't" and "I'm not good enough" echoes in your mind. They're like invisible chains, keeping you from reaching your full potential.

To identify your limiting beliefs, try this simple exercise:

1. Grab a piece of paper and a pen.

2. Write down any negative thoughts you have about yourself.

3. Look for patterns. Do you see any themes?

Once you've got your list, it's time to challenge these beliefs. Ask yourself:

- Is this really true?

- What evidence do I have that contradicts this belief?

- How is this belief serving me?

You might be surprised to find that many of these beliefs don't hold up under scrutiny. They're often based on past experiences or things others have said to us, not on current reality.

Creating Affirmations That Resonate

Now that we've identified those limiting beliefs, it's time to replace them with something more empowering. Enter affirmations, which are positive statements that can help re-shape your thinking.

But here's the thing: generic affirmations like "I am awesome" often fall flat. To really make an impact, your affirmations need to resonate with you personally.

Here's how to create powerful, personalized affirmations:

1. Start with "I am" or "I can."

2. Make it specific to your goals and values.

3. Use present tense, as if it's already true.

4. Keep it positive.

5. Make it believable (stretch yourself, but don't go too far).

For example, instead of "I am successful," try "I am capable of achieving my goals and learning from challenges along the way."

The goal isn't to lie to yourself. It's to focus on positive truths and possibilities that you might be overlooking.

Evidence-Based Techniques to Internalize New Beliefs

Creating affirmations is a great start, but how do we make them stick? Let's look at some evidence-based techniques to help internalize these new, empowering beliefs.

1. Visualization: Close your eyes and imagine yourself embodying your affirmation. What does it look like? How does it feel? The more vivid you can make this mental image, the more powerful it becomes.

2. Mirror Work: Stand in front of a mirror, look yourself in the eye, and say your affirmation out loud. It might feel awkward at first, but stick with it. This technique helps create a stronger connection between your words and your self-image.

3. Journaling: Write about times when you've demonstrated the qualities in your affirmation. This helps build evidence to support your new belief.

4. Celebrate Small Wins: Notice and celebrate moments when you act in alignment with your new belief. This reinforces the neural pathways associated with your desired mindset.

5. Surround Yourself with Support: Share your new beliefs with supportive friends or family. Ask them to point out when they see you embodying these qualities.

Remember, changing your mindset is a process. Be patient with yourself and keep at it. Over time, these new beliefs will become second nature.

John's Journey: From Self-Doubt to Self-Belief

Let's look at how this process played out for John, a marketing executive who struggled with imposter syndrome.

John had always been a high achiever, but deep down, he constantly felt like he wasn't good enough. This limiting belief showed up in various ways:

- He second-guessed his decisions at work.

- He was reluctant to speak up in meetings.

- He often worked late, trying to prove his worth.

One day, after missing out on a promotion, John decided it was time for a change. He started by identifying his core limiting belief: "I'm not good enough."

John challenged this belief by looking at his track record. He consistently met or exceeded his targets, received positive feedback from colleagues, and even won an industry award. The evidence clearly showed he was, in fact, quite good at his job.

Next, John created a personalized affirmation: "I am a skilled professional who brings valuable insights to my team and our clients."

To internalize this new belief, John:

- Visualized himself confidently leading meetings and pitching ideas.

- Practiced saying his affirmation in the mirror each morning.

- Kept a "wins" journal where he recorded his daily successes, no matter how small.

- Asked a trusted colleague to give him feedback when they saw him demonstrating confidence and skill.

At first, it felt forced. John's inner critic would pipe up, telling him he was being arrogant or fooling himself. But John persisted.

Slowly but surely, things began to change. John started speaking up more in meetings. He began to trust his instincts on projects. He even volunteered to lead a major client presentation, something he would have shied away from before.

Six months later, John's boss called him into her office. She had noticed a positive change in John's performance and attitude. She offered him a leadership role on an exciting new project.

John's journey wasn't always smooth. There were days when self-doubt crept back in. But now, he had the tools to manage these moments. He knew how to challenge his limiting beliefs and reinforce his inner champion.

The most significant change wasn't in John's external success (though that certainly improved). It was in how he felt about himself. He no longer felt like an imposter. He felt capable, worthy, and excited about his potential.

Your Turn to Shine

John's story shows us that transforming your inner critic into your biggest fan is possible. It takes time and effort, but the results can be life-changing.

Here's your action plan:

1. Identify your limiting beliefs.

2. Challenge them with evidence.

3. Create personalized, resonant affirmations.

4. Use evidence-based techniques to internalize your new beliefs.

5. Celebrate your progress, no matter how small.

Remember, you're not trying to silence your inner critic completely. That voice can sometimes offer valuable insights. The goal is to balance it with a strong, supportive inner champion.

You have greatness within you. It's time to let it shine. Start forging your inner champion mindset today, and watch as new possibilities open up in your life.

Habits That Shape Your Best Self

Ever wonder why some people seem to maintain their goals effortlessly while others struggle? The secret lies in their habits. Habits are the small, consistent actions that shape our lives and, ultimately, our identities. Let's explore how you can use habits to become the person you want to be.

Morning Rituals: Setting the Stage for Success

How you start your day can set the tone for everything that follows. A powerful morning ritual can reinforce your new identity and prime you for success. Here's how to create one:

1. Wake up early: Give yourself extra time to focus on your personal growth before the day's demands kick in.

2. Hydrate: Drink a glass of water to jumpstart your body and mind.

3. Move your body: Even a short stretch or quick workout can energize you and reinforce your "healthy self" identity.

4. Meditate or journal: Spend a few minutes in quiet reflection or writing. This helps clarify your thoughts and intentions for the day.

5. Affirm your identity: Say your personalized affirmations out loud or write them down.

6. Review your goals: Remind yourself of what you're working towards.

The key is consistency, not perfection. Start small and build up over time. Even a 10-minute morning ritual can make a big difference.

Habit Stacking: Building New Behaviors

Now, let's talk about a powerful technique called habit stacking. This involves attaching a new habit to an existing one, making it easier to remember and stick to.

Here's how it works:

1. Identify a current habit you do consistently (like brushing your teeth).

2. Choose a new habit you want to build.

3. Link the new habit to the existing one.

For example, if you want to start a gratitude practice, you might decide to think of three things you're grateful for while brushing your teeth each morning.

The formula is simple: "After ***, I will ***."

Some more examples:

- "After I pour my morning coffee, I will do 10 push-ups."

- "After I sit down at my desk, I will take three deep breaths."

- "After I get into bed, I will read for 10 minutes."

Habit stacking works because it uses the momentum of an existing habit to build a new one. It's like piggybacking on your current routines to create positive change.

Visualization and Mental Rehearsal

Your mind is a powerful tool in shaping your identity. By regularly visualizing yourself as the person you want to become, you can actually rewire your brain to support this new identity.

Here's a simple visualization exercise:

1. Find a quiet place where you won't be disturbed.

2. Close your eyes and take a few deep breaths.

3. Imagine yourself as the person you want to be. What are you doing? How do you carry yourself? How do you interact with others?

4. Engage all your senses. What do you see, hear, feel, smell, and taste in this vision?

5. Allow yourself to feel the positive emotions associated with this new identity.

6. Open your eyes and carry this feeling with you into your day.

Practice this visualization for 5-10 minutes daily. Over time, you'll find it easier to embody your desired identity in real life.

Mental rehearsal takes this a step further. Before important events or challenging situations, take a few minutes to walk through the scenario mentally. Imagine yourself handling it with confidence and skill, aligned with your new identity.

This technique is used by top athletes, performers, and business leaders to improve their performance and confidence. By practicing in your mind, you're preparing yourself for success in reality.

Maria's 30-Day Challenge: Becoming "Fit and Healthy"

Let's look at how these concepts played out in real life with Maria's story.

Maria had always struggled with her weight and energy levels. She wanted to see herself as a "fit and healthy" person, but her habits didn't match this identity. She decided to take on a 30-day challenge to align her actions with her desired self.

Here's what Maria did:

1. Morning Ritual: Maria set her alarm 30 minutes earlier. She started each day with a glass of water and 10 minutes of yoga, and she said her affirmation: "I am fit, healthy, and full of energy."

2. Habit Stacking: Maria linked new habits to existing ones:

- After brushing her teeth, she would do 10 squats.

- After sitting down at her desk, she would drink a glass of water.

- After dinner, she would go for a 15-minute walk.

3. Visualization: Each night before bed, Maria spent 5 minutes visualizing herself as fit and healthy. She imagined how she looked, how she felt, and the activities she enjoyed.

The first week was tough. Maria's body resisted the early mornings, and her mind doubted whether she could really change. But she persisted.

By the second week, things got easier. Maria found herself looking forward to her morning yoga. Her energy levels started to improve.

In the third week, Maria noticed she was naturally making healthier food choices. She felt more confident and started suggesting active outings with friends.

By the end of the 30 days, Maria was amazed at the changes. She had lost some weight, but more importantly, she felt different. She felt like the fit and healthy person she had visualized.

The challenge was over, but Maria kept up her new habits. They had become part of who she was.

Your Turn: Shaping Your Best Self

Maria's story shows how powerful habits can be in shaping our identity. Here's how you can apply these principles to become your best self:

1. Define your desired identity: Who do you want to be? What qualities do you want to embody?

2. Create a morning ritual: Design a simple routine that reinforces your new identity.

3. Use habit stacking: Identify 2-3 new habits you want to build and link them to existing routines.

4. Practice visualization: Spend a few minutes each day imagining yourself as your ideal self.

5. Be consistent: Remember, it's not about perfection. Small, consistent actions add up over time.

6. Track your progress: Keep a journal or use a habit-tracking app to monitor your new behaviors.

7. Celebrate small wins: Acknowledge your progress, no matter how small. This reinforces your new identity and motivates you to keep going.

Remember, becoming your best self is a journey, not a destination. There will be setbacks and challenges along the way. But with consistent habits aligned with your desired identity, you'll find yourself naturally becoming the person you want to be.

Your habits shape your identity, and your identity shapes your life. By consciously choosing habits that support your best self, you're not just changing what you do; you're changing who you are.

So, what habits will you start today to shape your best self? The power is in your hands. Take that first small step, and watch as it leads to big changes in your life and identity.

Nurturing Allies for Your Authentic Self

You've heard the saying, "You're the average of the five people you spend the most time with." While that might be an oversimplification, there's no denying the powerful influence our social circle has on our identity and success. Let's see how you can surround yourself with allies who support and reinforce your authentic self.

Seeking out Mentors and Role Models

Mentors and role models can be game-changers in your personal growth journey. They're like living, breathing examples of who you want to become. Here's how to find and connect with them:

1. Identify your goals: What aspects of your life do you want to improve? This will help you pinpoint the kind of mentor you need.

2. Look in your existing network: Sometimes, the perfect mentor is hiding in plain sight. It could be a colleague, a friend's parent, or someone you admire from afar.

3. Attend events and conferences: These are great places to meet potential mentors in your field of interest.

4. Use social media wisely: Follow people who inspire you. Engage with their content meaningfully.

5. Be bold and reach out: Many successful people are willing to help if asked respectfully. Don't be afraid to send that email or LinkedIn message.

Mentorship doesn't always have to be formal. Sometimes, a single conversation can provide insights that change your life.

Joining Communities Aligned with Your Aspirations

Want to accelerate your growth? Surround yourself with people who are on a similar journey. Here's how:

1. Online communities: Look for Facebook groups, Reddit forums, or specialized platforms in your area of interest.

2. Local meetups: Use platforms like Meetup.com to find groups in your area that align with your goals.

3. Professional associations: Many industries have associations that offer networking opportunities and resources.

4. Classes or workshops: Learning new skills puts you in contact with like-minded individuals.

5. Volunteer: Giving back not only feels good but also connects you with people who share your values.

Being part of a community provides support, accountability, and opportunities for collaboration. It's like having a whole team cheering you on.

Communicating Your Identity Shift to Friends and Family

As you evolve, it's important to communicate your changes to those closest to you. This can be tricky, but here are some tips:

1. Be clear about your intentions: Explain why this change is important to you.

2. Show, don't just tell: Let your actions demonstrate your new identity.

3. Be patient: Remember that it might take time for others to adjust to the "new you."

4. Set boundaries if needed: If some relationships are hindering your growth, it's okay to create some distance.

5. Invite them on your journey: Share your excitement and see if they want to join you in some of your new activities.

Your growth might inspire others, but be prepared for some resistance, too. Not everyone will understand or support your changes right away, and that's okay.

Tristan's Transformation Through a Mastermind Group

Let's look at how these principles played out for Tristan, a budding entrepreneur.

Tristan had always dreamed of starting his own business, but he felt stuck in his 9-to-5 job. He identified as a "worker bee," someone who followed orders rather than gave them. This identity was holding him back from taking the leap into entrepreneurship.

One day, Tristan stumbled upon a local entrepreneur meetup. Nervous but excited, he decided to attend. At the meetup, he met Mandy, a successful business owner who took him under her wing. Mandy became Tristan's mentor, offering advice and encouragement.

Inspired by the meetup, Tristan joined a mastermind group of aspiring entrepreneurs. The group met weekly to set goals, share challenges, and hold each other accountable. Here's what happened:

- Week 1-4: Tristan felt out of his depth. Everyone seemed more knowledgeable and confident. But he pushed through the discomfort and kept showing up.

- Week 5-8: Tristan started to contribute more. He realized his corporate experience gave him unique insights that others found valuable.

- Week 9-12: Tristan launched his side hustle, a consulting service. The group cheered him on and offered practical advice.

- Week 13-16: Tristan's business started to gain traction. He began to see himself as an entrepreneur, not just a dreamer.

Throughout this process, Tristan had to have some tough conversations with friends and family. Some were supportive, while others expressed concern about him leaving his stable job. Tristan explained his vision and invited them to be part of his journey.

By the end of four months, Tristan had transformed. He no longer saw himself as just an employee. He was an entrepreneur, a risk-taker, and a creator. His new identity gave him the courage to quit his job and eventually focus on his business full-time.

The mastermind group continued to be a source of support and inspiration. Tristan even became a mentor to newer members, further reinforcing his new identity.

Recap of Key Points

- Identity plays a crucial role in behavior change and personal growth. By changing how you see yourself, you change how you act.

- Crafting empowering beliefs is essential for overcoming self-doubt. Replace limiting thoughts with affirming ones.

- Daily practices reinforce and embody your ideal self. Consistency in small actions leads to big changes.

- A supportive environment accelerates your identity transformation. Surround yourself with people who believe in your potential.

Action Steps

1. Identify one limiting belief and create a corresponding empowering belief. For example, change "I'm not creative" to "I have unique ideas to offer the world."

2. Implement a daily practice that aligns with your desired identity. If you want to be a writer, commit to writing 100 words every day.

3. Reach out to someone who embodies the identity you aspire to and request a conversation. Be specific about what you admire and what you hope to learn.

As we've explored the power of identity in transforming your life, it's time to turn our attention to another crucial aspect of personal growth: resilience. In the conclusion, we'll reflect on all the things you've learned throughout the book to ensure that your newfound identity can withstand life's challenges.

Remember, becoming your authentic self is a journey, not a destination. There will be ups and downs, but with the right mindset, habits, and support system, you can become the person you've always known you could be. Your transformation starts now. Are you ready to take the next step?

Conclusion

Conclusion: Embracing Your Confident Self

As we reach the end of this transformative journey, let's take a moment to reflect on how far you've come. Remember that feeling when you first picked up this book? That spark of hope, that recognition of untapped potential within yourself? That same potential is still there, stronger than ever, waiting for you to fully embrace it.

You've learned so much along the way:

- Self-doubt isn't an immovable mountain - it's a challenge you can overcome.

- Your inner critic can become your biggest cheerleader.

- You have the power to rewrite your story and step into your most authentic, confident self.

Let's recap some of the key ideas we've explored together:

1. The Surprising Truth About Your Inner Saboteur

We uncovered the sneaky ways our minds try to hold us back. But now you know - that voice of doubt isn't the real you. It's just an old pattern you can change.

2. Turning Your Inner Critic into Your Biggest Fan

Remember those techniques for transforming negative self-talk? You've got the tools to make your inner voice a source of encouragement and strength.

3. The Procrastination Paradox

Procrastination doesn't have to be your enemy. You've learned how to harness that energy and turn delay into a powerful tool for success.

4. Failure as Your North Star

Failure isn't the opposite of success; it's a crucial part of the journey. Each setback is a stepping stone guiding you forward.

5. The Gratitude Revolution

You've discovered how shifting from scarcity to abundance can transform your entire outlook on life.

6. Mindfulness for the Skeptic

Even in your busiest moments, you now have practical ways to stay present and centered.

7. The Nutrition-Confidence Connection

Who knew that what you eat could have such a big impact on how you feel about yourself? You're now armed with knowledge to nourish your body and your confidence.

8. Boundary Alchemy

You've learned the art of saying "no" to make room for bigger "yeses" in your life.

9. Your Personal Board of Directors

You understand the power of surrounding yourself with the right people. Your inner circle can lift you higher than you ever thought possible.

10. The 'What If' Game

Your imagination is a superpower. You know how to use it to fuel your dreams instead of your fears.

11. Action Alchemy

Small steps lead to big changes. You've got the blueprint for turning tiny actions into life-changing momentum.

12. The Identity Shift

You're no longer stuck with old labels. You have the power to become the person you've always wanted to be.

The most important takeaways? Here they are:

- Everyone doubts themselves sometimes. It's not a flaw; it's part of being human.

- Confidence is like a muscle. The more you work it, the stronger it gets.

- Your thoughts shape your world. Choose them carefully.

- When you're scared, take action. It's the best cure for fear.

- Messing up isn't failing. It's learning.

- Take care of your body. It's the home of your confidence.

- Hang out with people who believe in you. Their faith will rub off on you.

- Picture your success, then make it happen.

- Get comfy with being uncomfortable. That's where the magic happens.

So what's next? I've got a challenge for you. For the next 30 days, commit to your confidence:

Week 1: Start and end each day by writing down three things you're grateful for. Add one thing you like about yourself.

Week 2: Pick one task you've been putting off. Break it into tiny steps. Do one step each day, no matter how small.

Week 3: Do one thing every day that scares you a little. It could be as simple as saying hi to a stranger or trying a new food.

Week 4: Reach out to one person each day who makes you feel good about yourself. Thank them for being in your life.

Throughout the month:

- Keep a record of your small wins. Celebrate them!

- Check in with yourself every Sunday. What's working? What needs to change?

- Find a friend to do this with you. Support each other.

- At the end of 30 days, look back at how far you've come. Then, set some new goals!

As we wrap up, I want you to know something: I believe in you. The fact that you picked up this book, that you stuck with it, and that you're ready to change already shows how strong you are.

The road to confidence isn't always smooth. There will be bumps and turns. But every challenge is a chance to grow. Every setback teaches you something new. And every little win proves how tough you really are.

You've got everything you need to create the life you dream about. Be patient with yourself. Be kind to yourself. And never forget you can do amazing things.

Your journey is just beginning. Go out there with your head held high. Be your true self. Build that awesome life you deserve. The world is waiting for you to shine.

Believe in yourself. I do.

Now go get 'em!